DISPOSABLE ANIMALS

ENDING THE TRAGEDY

OF

THROWAWAY PETS

Craig Brestrup

Camino Bay Books   Kendalia, Texas

Camino Bay Books
331 Old Blanco Road
Kendalia, TX 78027
(830)336-3636 ~ (800)463-8181
fax (830)336-3635

Cover design by Nigel Pickhardt and Dale Wilkins.
Back cover photo © 1992 by Jodi Frediani.

First edition.

Second printing 2002.

Publisher's Cataloging-in-Publication Data

Brestrup, Craig, 1945-
    Disposable animals: ending the tragedy of throwaway pets/
Craig Brestrup
        p.   cm.
    Includes bibliographical references and index.
1. Animal welfare—Moral and ethical aspects. 2. Animal rights. 3.
Animal shelters. 4. Euthanasia of animals. 5. Pets—Social aspects. II.
Title.
HV4708.B74 1997
179.3—dc21   97-66622
ISBN 0-9657285-9-5

TO

Supporters, Volunteers, Staff, and Board
at
Progressive Animal Welfare Society
Lynnwood, Washington.

Through such people as these
and a few more like them,
a proper respect for our fellow animals
will one day prevail.

Universal Declaration of the Rights of Animals
    Item 1: All animals are born with an equal claim on
            life and the same rights to existence.
    Item 2: All companion animals have the right to
            complete their natural life span.

    International League of the Rights of Animals (1977)

~

We realize it is a necessary kindness to put to sleep unwanted animals.

    Humane Society Official

CONTENTS

ACKNOWLEDGMENTS

After a year's work writing the first draft of this book, I knew it needed critical review by fresh eyes. Since I intended it chiefly for two categories of readers—people working in animal-related endeavors and people qualified simply by virtue of particular care and commitment to animals—I sought advice and criticism from both these groups. Most were generous in offering their thoughts, and this is the place to publicly repeat what I have already privately communicated, for the truth is that while bylines carry but one or a few names every book arises as a collective expression, the result of countless conversations through a variety of mediums.

Beth Perrine, a friend of uncommon discernment and sensitivity to her fellow creatures, responded to the manuscript first, and I appreciated both her insights and support. As speaker of the initial kind words, she moderated my anxieties.

Mitchell Fox, Director of Animal Advocacy for the Progressive Animal Welfare Society and former valued colleague there, not only read the manuscript and critiqued it but guided me to others of his acquaintance from within the animal welfare/rights field for comment as well. He has worked long and effectively for all manner of animals, from kittens to apes, and was instrumental in putting together the working group who used some of the book as catalyst and point of departure in attempts to arouse new energy among workers in companion animal welfare.

He led me to Kim Sturla of The Fund for Animals and Animal Place sanctuary, who also participated in the group and provided input and inspiration, and to Ed Sayres of the American Humane Association, who became a collaborator in our efforts.

Dr. Tom Regan, animal rights leader and thoughtful scholar, provided the early suggestions that led to radically restructuring my approach to the book so that it could become more useful and readable (as I hope it has). Ingrid Newkirk, President of People for the Ethical Treatment of Animals, read that first draft and forcefully reminded me that some will disagree with my views of true welfare for companion animals, as did she. Others who encouraged and/ or advised: Cleveland Amory, President of The Fund for Animals; Dr. Jeffrey Morris, board member at PAWS and recycling/resource management guru; and Jeanne Wasserman, Director of PAWS' wildlife rehabilitation center and bright good friend who took time to extensively and helpfully comment. Finally, my thanks to Ed Duvin, now at In Defense of Animals and the person in 1989 who first forcefully raised the issues challenging "euthanasia's" efficacy for the protection and welfare of animals. He was much maligned but carries on, articulate and gentle man that he is.

INTRODUCTION

On the first of February 1994 I entered a realm completely new to me. After twenty years in mental health, first as psychotherapist and then chief executive of counseling clinics, I became executive director of an organization devoted to animals: wildlife rehabilitation, sheltering and adoption of companion animals, and advocacy activities for animal rights. The experiences that allowed me into this milieu were my years as an administrator and a doctorate received five years earlier in medical humanities with a concentration in medical and environmental ethics. That study had arisen out of a declining fascination with the variabilities of human psyches and a concomitant arousal to nature and animals.

My expectation on entering the new field was that animal rights and wildlife would be my primary program interests. Philosophical work in animal rights and a personal affinity and anxiety for wildlife predicted it, despite my lifelong involvement with dogs. *Canis familiaris* after all is, well, familiar, even prosaic, beloved though he is. Cats, too.

But I was wrong in that expected focus.

Among the Search Committee's preinterview written inquiries, resting innocently among questions about animal experimentation, vegetarianism, and the myriad uses to which we put animals, from zoos to rodeos, was this: "What is the candidate's opinion about animal shelter euthanasia of surplus, homeless companion animals?" I had never given the matter much thought. Looking across the room at my dog Annie, a shelter-derived creature herself, I was abashed. That she could have been killed merely for lack of a home or a place to keep her until one could be found felt wrong. Nevertheless, glib with conventional wisdom (I see retrospectively), I responded that it seemed a great tragedy and I earnestly hoped that such action would be taken only as the very last resort, but that humane termination of a life with no place for living must be a necessity. In light of the overflowing canine and feline populations, it seemed a reasonable response. I put it down and sent it on and was eventually offered the job. I took it, trading muffled sounds of human fury and tears through my former office walls for barks and howls and clanging kennel gates through my new ones.

Before long I realized that my answer to the euthanasia question was insufficient. It nagged at me continually. I read all that I could find and discussed it at length with both supporters and opponents. I was surprised to find that shelter workers, the people who take care of the animals and who make the selections and perform the euthanasias, are among the strongest proponents of the practice. Finally, my internal process could no longer be denied, and I spent a weekend writing about the ethics and pragmatics of euthanasia as best I could fathom them. The essay concluded with a recommendation that we cease the practice and focus on all other imaginable ways of responding to and solving companion animal overpopulation.

I distributed the essay to staff for discussion and found that it aroused enormous controversy. Shelter workers opposed it, and most of the other employees were either favorable or undecided. Then it went to the board program committee and after much struggle to the full board of directors with the committee's affirmative recommendation. More struggle, and the board assented. We replaced the shelter workers who resigned in protest and moved ahead with an eleven-month deadline for ending killing that is not euthanasia in the strict sense.

Part One of what follows is my attempt to more deeply understand this issue, to parse and critique its many facets and implications, to identify connections with other cultural practices, and to suggest alternatives. I am as objective in the assessment as I can be without wanting or pretending to scholarly aloofness. I intend to advocate. I want every animal welfarist and protectionist, liberationist and rightist, and the organizations for which they labor to reject this killing of healthy animals. We can and must do better than that—and the animals deserve better.

I want to say something here to those who work in animal shelters even though recent experience tells me that it will be rejected. But I must say it anyway. Nothing within this work is intended to demean those who have made the conscientious decision that "euthanasia" is often the only compassionate choice available to them in the animal over-populated world in which we currently live. Their care for the animals coming through shelters and their pain at the execution of the choice they have made are unquestioned. I simply think it a wrong choice, just as many of them consider mine. I have seen how easy it is for the debate to become personalized, and I find that sad and distracting from the serious work we have to do. Analogous to the situation twenty-five or so years ago, when many of us challenged the Viet Nam War and resisted the draft, I primarily oppose the policy and policy-makers, not those on the lines struggling to do right.

Of course, there would be no stimulus for this effort, no enigma to examine, and no dilemma for animal caretakers, were it not for participants not yet mentioned. The truly guilty, being the source of the problem, are those who choose to have animals without choosing to do so in a morally responsible way. That way would be to recognize the value inherent in the life of an animal and to actively respect it, to take charge of its reproduction, to recognize that to take in an animal is to take on a relationship of commitment for his or her lifetime. When we achieve that vision, the killing simply stops.

Part Two consists of essays on human relations with other animals in settings outside home or animal shelter. I decided to include them in this book, where the focus is primarily on contingencies faced by companion animals, because the situations of wild and companion animals are connected, and I want to encourage awareness of that fact. As nonhumans both are assigned categories of existential inferiority which culminates in moral inferiority—not so low as plants and stones but far beneath our own exalted status. So when companion animals become surplus, due to *our* failures to be responsible, we kill *them.* In the wild, we kill recreationally; in the laboratory, we subject them to experimentation; at the factory farm...; at the dinner table...; and so on. Too many of us only see objects where inherently valuable life resides. Further, we contradict ourselves when we claim respect for animals in their dog and cat incarnations while exploiting the others for profit, pleasure, food, and other such purposes.

Part Three describes an exploration I undertook during the preparation of what became Part One. It presents more detail than earlier regarding ways in which companion animal devaluation and "euthanasia" mirror prevailing attitudes toward nature, other animals, and the self. All things connect and cultural prescriptions for acceptable behavior and laudable aspiration ramify throughout, creating in the Western instance at least, casualties all along the way—nature and animals among them. The section concludes with a version of an ethic that differs greatly from prevailing practice, but which I find persuasive and friendlier toward life, human *and* other-than-human.

The upshot throughout is simple: humanity shares Earth, and both justice and responsibility require that we respect the legitimate claims of other life. After all, without the company of that life—microbes to mammals—we would be abjectly lonely, and not around for long.

PART ONE

COMPANION ANIMAL WELFARE
RECONSIDERED

1

THE ANIMAL SHELTER

Prologue: Speaking to the Source

Without crime there would be no need for a mushrooming criminal justice system: police, courts, jails, judges, lawyers, and all the other personnel, equipment, and facilities necessary to maintain and monitor our population of criminals.

Similarly, without that population of people who want the pleasures of animal companionship but who falter in the responsibilities, there would be no need for the organized practice of animal welfare: animal control departments, animal shelters, and all the people who work in these areas and who face daily the terrible dilemma of how best to meet the needs of animals abandoned, of animals superfluous. While crime is a legal construct that so far only marginally provides standing for animal victims, the negligence leading to homeless animals is a moral failure and as such remains mostly within the arena of conscience for remediation. We have to ask perpetrators: How is it that by the millions annually you neglect responsibility for a relationship chosen by you but where the chief consequences of failure are displaced on to the one you chose?

We live in a commodity-centered culture, one which degrades almost everything it touches through this dominant orientation. Animals, too, are commoditized, and that provides the context for moral failure. But individuals make the choice—to affirm or reject a cultural practice—and it merits a close look to see what personal considerations permit and direct that choice.

Self-centeredness must be the first characteristic involved in disregard for the animal, and we can add to that human-centeredness. The first of these acts as if self-gratification supersedes the interests of any others, and the second believes the same, only it elevates human interests above those of all other kinds of creatures. These together allow little room for concern for the animal for her own sake, but only insofar as she is of use to the human owner. Empathy, the willingness to imagine what things are like from the animal's perspective, hardly exists among these self-involved people.

A man brings his cat to the shelter. She has lived with him for eight years. She is an attractive example of an unusual breed and once flattered his sense of himself as an exotic personality. But he has redecorated, she sheds, the color scheme fails to disguise it anymore, he will not be bothered to groom her, and he has discovered a short-haired exemplar of a more unusual breed. He hopes the shelter can find her a good home, and then he leaves.

Relationships, whether with cats or people, do not flourish in atmospheres heavy with egocentrism. Ours is an individualistic society, and there is much good in that. But individualism always risks falling into excessive self-regard. Mutuality and obligation can seem burdensome and unacceptable infringements on an individual's wants. That cat had become inconvenient, and without empathy and commitment her companion saw no reason to stand by her under changed conditions.

Part of the sadness of excessive self-involvement arises as the self separates from both its nonegocentric needs and from the others around him. Such separation paves the way for another damaging perception of animals: their objectification. In this sense they are seen as objects lacking inherent value. The animal's worth and demand for respect decreases with the elevation of self. She becomes an object alongside other consummable objects for keeping and tending only so long as convenient and useful. The separated one fails to notice the animal as a creature of needs, feelings, and attachments. She represents a diversion, a symbol, a disposable.

Animal control brings a medium-sized mixed-breed dog to the shelter door. He bleeds from encounter with a car, has scars from fights, is malnourished and badly frightened. His story can be readily surmised. A back- yard animal, rarely related to and erratically tended, protected by no or inadequate fencing, he is merely an impulse, a supposed watchdog, an object. And now he has become so aggressive and unsocialized that adoption is hardly imaginable. To his supposed guardian he never quite existed as more than an obscure presence on the periphery of attention. That person almost certainly will not appear at the shelter searching for the dog, and if by chance he did it would only postpone the inevitable for the unfortunate and neglected animal.

Self-absorption, along with objectification, allows a host of derelictions found in the treatment of companion animals. Together these point to the depletion of care and responsibility in the individual's relation to the world outside his skin. Together they also reveal the acceptability of such behavior, its inevitability, really, within the dominant context of striving. Such imbalance between self and other can lead nowhere else. So clear-cut forestry, industrial toxification of air and water, children de facto sacrificed to the economy, the gospel of ever-escalating desire, abandonment of the animals—all these and much more are rooted in the enthronement of self and wealth combined with the debasement of others.

People with animals are called "owners." A century and a half ago, people with slaves were owners. In the relation of one life to another, ownership is not a beneficial framework, for something owned lacks an autonomous center of value. While that fits for an automobile, it does not for a life. An entity owned can only serve the wants of the owner and not claim its own priorities. An owned animal becomes a consumer item, disposable and replaceable as all such items are, and not a locus for commitment. The notion of companionship, rather than ownership, offers a more promising ideal for the mutuality of one life with another. The nature of things requires that the human side of the companionship carries responsibilities and freedoms not possible for the nonhuman side. The human, however, is not released from the obligation to take care of the one taken in, who is not, after all, a commodity.

A woman arrives at the animal shelter with a purebred dog at the end of her leash, a German Shepherd bought through a pet store. He had been expected to make her feel safer in living alone, but hip dysplasia, overaggressiveness, and a variety of chronic health problems made him a disappointment instead. She has found another, at another store, guaranteed this time, and she expects the shelter to relieve her of the burden of her error. The fate of that "mistake" is one she prefers not to know. The animal, a flawed artifact of artificial selection (selection certainly not with his welfare in mind), like other damaged goods has been replaced.

Some bought animals, like other consumer items, carry a freight of symbolism on their backs. The man who wants a wolf hybrid or pit bull or the woman with a clipped and beribboned "designer" dog may be telling us something about who they wish to be. As cars and jewelry are advertised in a way that promises personal transformation through possession, these animals are expected to foster well-being by association. They are stylish, but styles change.

Other animals are expected to be the source of a loving relationship not otherwise available to the human. Substitutes for what's really wanted, creatures of imagination rather than flesh and blood, they remain always vulnerable to replacement by one more promising (or intolerant or jealous).

Consumption as a world view and life style (not the sometimes necessary, occasionally enhancing, but always secondary activity) thrives upon misconception. It promises ready access—purchasable access—to transcendence and expansion of self, to status and self-respect, to fullness of being—all good and important experiences that by their nature can be earned but not bought. Animals thrust into the role of consumer goods will eventually disappoint as their reality comes through or as other passing imagery seizes the consumers' hopes. Then they are turned in to the shelter (like an unread book to the library) and to a most uncertain and often foreshortened future.

A mother and child enter and see a sign saying "animal

adoptions" over one counter and "animal receiving" over another. She carries a box resounding with plaintive kitten meows and heads to the second sign. There are four, two having been found homes in the neighborhood, with mother cat grieving at home and still fertile. This is the cat's third litter, seventeen living kittens, in just over a year. Many end up adopted, but each fortunate one displaces a waiting, homeless adult who ends up dead to "euthanasia" for lack of space or a home to take him. The box-carrying mother appears sheepish; she has been admonished to spay the animal after earlier deliveries. However, her resolve departs with the kittens and as other matters capture her attention.

There is ignorance in this. Could she be expected to know about the thousand "surplus" animals across the nation who died in the time it took her to drive to the shelter and leave her full box, or the other 30,000 or so who will die by the same time tomorrow for the mistake of being surplus within our borders? She has been told this before, in so many words, but it seems unreal. She does not see the bodies. Besides, she has so many other things to think about.

There is also a lack of empathy. If we are obliged to do anything in this life it must be to pay attention, to use senses and intuition, to be aware and to respond accordingly. We damage those things we affect unfeelingly. What is it like to live in a cage in a strange place, surrounded by anxious animals and unfamiliar people, approached and repeatedly stepped away from by strangers, and perhaps aware that death lies just around the corner? The connection between what the person does at home about that fertile cat and what happens at the shelter to all those other cats is invisible but real and effective, and deadly.

Then comes another dog to the shelter, an energetic one-year-old who entertains himself through shoe chewing and hole digging. His guardians have tried keeping him both inside and out without change in his habits. He is alone eleven or so hours each day. Man and woman, his supposed companions, work long hours, lead busy lives, and do not have much energy left for him (or each other) when all else has been said and done. They had hoped he would be a relaxing diversion from the pressures, perhaps a surrogate for a never-conceived child, but instead he makes demands and has needs and does damage. They leave him with relief; he was a wrong choice and an extra stress. Maybe a cat will do.

And another is pulled through the door: companions moving to a "no pets" apartment. And another: allergies. Another: the kids will not take care of him. Another: she barks. Another: he scratches the furniture. Fleas. The expense. The boyfriend....

Only the range of human error limits the range of reasons for deserting animals. Maybe it's predictable; after all, half our marriages end in divorce. And child suffering climbs year after year. But we know these things are signs of something gone wrong: commitments that don't bind, that turn out not to have been commitments at all; preoccupation with externals, with the means of living at the expense of the meanings; a steep decline in the experience of wonder and gratitude at the sheer fact of life and of respect for its community of members. All this needs reexamination, and one place to begin is to study the relations people have with these animals. You ought not enter the relation casually. You define yourself by the where and how of your relations, in this case as much as anywhere else. Lives hinge on the definition. Do it right.

One Solution to the Problem

Just after 6:00 p.m. Jim approaches the chain link gate of the kennel that Sport has called home for the past four days. Shelter worker eyes shelter resident and Sport expectantly returns the look. He recognizes Jim, who passes by several times a day in the course of his duties and sometimes stops with words and touches. A glance at the clipboard confirms Jim's mission. He opens the gate, leashes the lonely dog, and walks the aisle past the other inmates. All of them are curious, and some bark with unknowing envy for Sport's apparent freedom and companionship. And Sport seems pleased, perhaps thinking he has another walk on the trail through the woods before sleep.

They depart the kennels through a door to the left, and after a few steps they turn right into a small white room that looks rather like a veterinarian's examination cubicle. It is not.

Sport was brought to the shelter by his owner. The form on Jim's clipboard offers scant information but it is all that remains of the dog's biography, the only potential biographer having abandoned him. A Lab/Australian sheep dog mix, he was acquired through a newspaper ad eight years ago, has always lived outside and slept in a shed, digs holes and barks at strangers. He has never been walked on a leash; he is ten years old. His owner moved to an apartment and said he could not afford the pet deposit. Sport belongs to the shelter now.

He is a friendly dog and, though old, adoptable in the abstract because he is healthy and companionable. Concretely, however, he is not handsome or prepossessing in any other way; and ten are a lot of dog years, particularly when up and down the aisle is an array of smaller, cuter, younger cohorts. Many visitors have looked at Sport but none has chosen him. Jim thinks the old dog gave up hoping two days ago. And now the white room.

Jim and Valerie are the technicians in charge tonight. They have worked with animals for years. At home both have more dogs and cats of their own than the law allows. They are knowledgeable about animal needs and behavior and consider their animals as emotionally important to them as their human friends. Genuine "animal lovers," they hate what they are about to do but are utterly convinced of its necessity and compassion.

Like others who perform "euthanasia," Jim and Valerie worked in the shelter for several months of acclimation before undergoing training, observing others, and finally doing it themselves under supervision. After hundreds of these deadly encounters, they are now experts.

Selections are based on two basic criteria. Unadoptable animals go first. This determination is based on health and behavior. Illness or viciousness are fatal liabilities. The second to go are adoptable, but space has run out. More animals are arriving than there are cages. Relative adoptability, based on such things as temperament, behavior, age, size, and appearance, becomes determinative. Days have passed with no one choosing to adopt Sport: he does not score well on adoptability and Jim was forced to select him. Valerie closes the door behind them.

Sport weighs close to fifty pounds so he remains on the floor. Valerie crouches beside him, speaking softly, even lovingly, in his ear. She places one hand firmly but gently under his jaw and with the other holds a front leg steady. He appears uneasy but does not resist her. A dog his size requires 5cc's of sodium pentobarbitol, and Jim has drawn this amount into a syringe with a one-inch needle. He ties off a vein with a tourniquet, shaves an area of the leg just below the elbow, inserts the needle into the vein, looks briefly into Sport's eyes, releases the tourniquet, and then quickly depresses the plunger. In five seconds the dog slumps unconscious in Valerie's arms, and in minutes Jim verifies his death: respiration has ceased, eye reflexes gone, heartbeat silenced. Over the hours rigor mortis will steal over the corpse. They gently lower Sport into a barrel, and Jim picks up his clipboard and returns to the kennels.

The season is spring, a time when not only flowers but also litters burst forth: it will be a busy night.

Sport was deserted by an owner who seemed after eight years neither to know nor care about him. Jim and Valerie coddled and cherished the dog, and after four days killed him. Had he been able, Sport might have wondered what all this meant about human values and relationships.

~

If "A foolish consistency is the hobgoblin of little minds," as Emerson noticed long ago, then surely a comparable inconsistency is worth close examination. You will find such at your Humane Society, Society for the Prevention of Cruelty to Animals, and most other animal care organizations.

Doctrinaire animal welfarists will protest the allegation. Killing unwanted animals is paradoxical and tragic, they will say, but certainly not foolish. And inconsistent only to the uninformed or naive. To my mind, though, it's a misplaced and macabre practice, and the victims' sorrowful eyes ask why. Why needles of ice blue fluid seeking veins for insertion? Why not people doing better than this?

I implied a foolish inconsistency, but that follows Emerson without quite capturing the thing. A fatal inconsistency is more like it: fatal in its impact on life and logic. The matter I struggle with is this: how can it be that the animals closest to us as companions and emotional sources and supports, dogs and cats, are deliberately killed annually by the millions? By, of all people, animal welfarists, people whose lives and careers are most deeply devoted to these ordinarily cherished creatures?

Origins

The first animal shelter in the United States (or Europe, for that matter) opened in 1874 "when Miss Elizabeth Morris of Philadelphia established quarters where unwanted, homeless, and injured cats and dogs could be humanely housed and destroyed....The work might even be traced back to 1858, when Miss Morris and Miss Annie Waln began their self-appointed task of picking up stray cats and dogs and chloroforming all they were unable to place in suitable homes." This bit of history appeared in a 1924 publication by Sydney Coleman, who spoke a few pages later of SPCA organizations: "The public is taught through a systematic campaign, by means of circulars and the press, where injured and unwanted animals could be disposed of. In this way thousands of animals are annually removed and painlessly destroyed, which would otherwise suffer from starvation and become a serious menace to public health."

Mr. Coleman's discussion is of a period beginning almost a century and a half ago and culminating three- quarters of a century before the present. Today's well-intended solution to the problem of companion animal overabundance remains the same, only the disposal method has changed.

Progress in this grisly problem-solving technology was described by Roswell McRae in 1910. Before 1894 in New York City, the dog pound, he said, "was a place of horror." Drowning was the method of choice, with clubbing in reserve for unfortunate survivors. Subsequent humanitarian sensibilities initiated "asphyxiation in an airtight chamber into which illuminating gas is introduced. In 1907, 108,619

DISPOSABLE ANIMALS

small animals were thus destroyed."

In Philadelphia, the Women's Pennsylvania Society for the Prevention of Cruelty to Animals did the job with carbonic oxide gas, which was "regarded as superior to illuminating gas on the score of humanity and efficiency." In 1908 they disposed of 88% of the dogs who came their way in this manner. (In 1995, nationwide about 67% of shelter animals were still sent off this mortal plane with humane attendance.)

In Boston in 1899 the Animal Rescue League was formed. Writing in 1924, William Schultz provided clear, if unintended, revelation of the problem's source in human irresponsibility and uncontrolled animal reproductivity. The League was a busy and growing organization. During non-summer seasons it sent agents into Boston's rural environs "to relieve the residents of the territory of their surplus pets." The ARL believed that in the absence of this service, which culminated in "humane disposal," many people would simply turn the animals out. In a similar vein, the League patrolled the beaches around Boston every October: "It has found that many families take dogs and cats with them to their summer homes at the beaches or else adopt strays during their stay there. When the time for departure arrives, no thought is given to these creatures. They are left to struggle to maintain life for a miserable month or two until they perish during the winter months." In 1921 League agents collected 401 such animals. "Our object," said their policy statement, "is to prevent and to release animals from suffering." Modern animal rescuers, seven and a half decades later, claim the same object, to the same effect.

Rationales

As described in the Introduction, the move away from killing healthy animals in my organization began with an essay. After its distribution to staff, some wrote responses which I draw upon for the following. Their comments were sometimes acerbic and angry but mostly thoughtful, seemingly pragmatic, and deeply opposed to ending "euthanasia." In their view it remains an essential element of compassionate animal care and sheltering.

One asked, "Is killing always incompatible with respect?"

Dogs and cats, she answered, are artifacts to about the same degree they are creatures of nature. Products of artificial selection over thousands of years, they no longer have a niche in the natural world and thus are uniquely vulnerable and dependent on humans. In essence, how it goes for them is almost completely a function of how it goes in their relationships with us.

Despite this radically contingent way of being, she continued, companion animals still have a core, an essence, a set of needs whose satisfaction is vital to their experience of a good life. Among these needs are sufficient and nurturant companionship, adequate food and shelter, and respectful treatment; in other words, a relationship that is nonexploitive, nonabusive, and that fosters insofar as possible the ways of being natural to their kind. Responsible ownership of an animal will honor all of these realities, and the person who will not honor them should not have an animal.

Shelters exist for those animals who are homeless because they are lost or unwanted. With luck someone will appear to reclaim the stray or to adopt the available. Except for self-declared "no-kill" shelters (traditionally scoffed at by mainstream shelter culture), it is an article of faith, source of pride, and guide for action that the shelter will never turn an animal away. This is known variously as the open-door policy, the safety net, the sanctuary concept. Shelter workers are well aware that the number of animals far exceeds the number of caring homes that are open to them, not to mention the number of spaces available in the shelter. But they see the world fraught with danger, suffering, and insult for companion animals and themselves as the major realm of protection. "In the shelter, we [staff] come to know them....And all of us in the shelter, who have this knowledge and understanding, believe that the killing of animals for whom there are no proper homes, is an act both merciful and respectful."

Another certainty in the minds of shelter workers is the vision of "fates worse than death" for the animals. Such fates disastrously violate the precepts described above: lives that deny their central being (for example, warehoused at a shelter or chained and ignored in someone's backyard), absence of proper care, a life of suffering, abuse, or neglect. Confronted with these ominous prospects and a surplus of animals, shelter people believe that "euthanasia," or "putting to sleep" (as it is still commonly referred to even among those who do it), is the compassionate and responsible obligation of those who care for them. Based on this, six to ten million will be killed this year (as they were last year and will again next), roughly seven percent of the number who live in homes. Proponents consider this tragic, abhorrent, even wrong in certain respects, but inescapable and humane. To challenge this exposes one's ignorance of companion animal reality and one's insensitivity to the feelings and commitments of those who care enough to do the work. It is, after all, a terrible and genuine dilemma that the very ones who kill these creatures are those most dedicated to their welfare.

A few years ago this issue flared into open debate within the animal caring community. Ed Duvin, publisher of a periodical named *animalines*, wrote an essay in 1989 entitled "In the Name of Mercy." Powerfully and almost unflinchingly presented, it mightily stirred the normally placid welfarist waters. Duvin's passion arose from his perception of shelters' performance shortcomings in relation to his view of their vital mission: "affirming the sanctity of life and Earth," preserving the lives of those millions of "precious beings" currently killed in shelters.

Among the failings he noted were these: 1) inadequate management practices, including data collection, quality control, and performance assessment; 2) lack of coordinated national efforts on behalf of animal protection; 3) educational initiatives that were both underaggressive and underfunded; 4) insufficient outreach and utilization of volunteers; and 5) reluctance to confront opposing interests such as animal breeders, veterinarians, and pet food manufacturers. Worst of all, he asserted, was the prevailing mentality, the acceptance and passivity before the "unconscionable death toll,....an assembly line of slaughter....[the definition of] their preeminent responsibility as preventing suffering rather than preserving life." Further, "it borders on the obscene to describe the killing of many millions of innocent and healthy beings as a merciful act....Euthanasia might be a relatively painless end to this journey of terror [through shelters]; but each death represents an abject failure—not an act of mercy."

Duvin's essay generated a profusion of angry responses, but I will draw from only one, for it comprehensively states the position and came from a person who characterized my organization's shift in similar terms. Since her thoughts were contained in a letter to Duvin, I will not identify her other than to say she was at that time an administrator with a state humane association and now holds a similar position with a national organization of the same sort.

On the one hand, she said, Duvin failed to appreciate the "enormous progress and extraordinary accomplishments" that had occurred among shelters. Nor, on the other, did he sufficiently appreciate the overwhelming operational tasks and challenges they faced daily. More public education would certainly be good, but much was being done already, resources were always limited, and in any event education was no panacea. Close to half her missive then followed in this vein: the goal of eliminating animal overpopulation was "probably illusory"; "ministering to those victims" via euthanasia was a vital task and therefore no failure; those who perform the task deserved better than to have him question it and by extension them; and the alternative "fates worse than death" qualified the practice as merciful.

Duvin spoke of "institutional inertia" among shelters and the preceding chants its mantra. Self-congratulatory for accomplishment, self-exculpatory for failure, it presents it all as operating under inexorable and probably eternal necessity. The same voice has been heard for decades. Meanwhile, perhaps 30,000 dogs and cats are killed in shelters every day, seven days a week.

Inconsistency

We see that defenders of "euthanasia" believe deeply in the practice, at least in its necessity and compassion. Now I want to portray some of the overlapping dimensions of the inconsistency I alluded to at the beginning. For the deaths appall me and the rationales behind them mystify me, particularly in their power to self-justify and to assuage the battered emotions of the participants who grimly clutch them.

Our site is the companion animal shelter and this is what happens. Every day countless dogs and cats arrive: unplanned litters, strays, as often as not "owner"-releases (that is, animals whose companions for a variety of usually shabby reasons have chosen to relinquish them). Never turned away, in numbers seeming without end, these animals keep shelters full almost always. The old, decrepit, ill, and emotionally and behaviorally disturbed will soon be euthanized. Even so, space always remains at a premium and the threshold for killing fluctuates with the numbers. On a crowded day a healthy animal (like Sport) who has been resident for a time without attracting an adoptive suitor will gently be led away toward chemical oblivion, never to return. A numbers game and a beauty contest—for lack of space to stay and time to wait, he lost. His consolation is this: No hands and hearts more caring could have accompanied him on this final journey. Shelter workers genuinely, deeply devote themselves to these animals. And at the end of the day, they kill them.

When I first encountered this phenomenon up close, I ambivalently accepted the explanations and sadly resigned myself to necessity. Like a late winter crocus, however, ambivalence grew and searched for light. Initially the stimulus was blatantly emotional. Faces, especially eyes of dogs, express astonishing feeling, particularly to one hypersensitized by a deadly knowledge. Among much else, they make a claim to exist, to continue on a course of life.

Pain—theirs and mine—stimulated questions and efforts to resolve them, intellectually if no other way. I experienced a massive case of cognitive dissonance, of confusion between means and ends. Animal advocates are the voices for animals. Not a single voice, certainly, they range from moderates who advocate kindliness in our relations with animals to liberationists and rightists who find it hard to discern much morally relevant difference between them and us. But in some measure nearly all affirm the intrinsic value of dog and cat and much other nonhuman life. These are not stones, after all, mere objects who turn their eyes to ours. They live, experience, and feel—and they give every indication of preferring to continue those activities. Animal welfarists believe all this and are eager to condemn the irresponsibility that fosters animal suffering.

All agree that companion animal overpopulation and its corollary homelessness represent blatant cultural failure. The result of undercommitment and deliberate and accidental overbreeding, and utterly preventable, it results sometimes in an overabundance of kittens and puppies, and always includes adult animals who are difficult to place in homes. For older animals, who lack the charm of youth, the problem is most severe. Additionally, the charm factor leads to impulsive acquisition of animals who grow bigger, less charming, or more obstreperous and who then find themselves deposited at the shelter. It drives shelter workers crazy, and for decades they have preached sermons on the need for guardians to act responsibly and to neuter their animals. Their words have had some, but not yet sufficient, success.

Here enters one version of the dissonance. Shelter welfarists condemn overpopulation and affirm intrinsic value—the animals matter and they deserve to live. Yet the shelter, like the last link in a recycling chain, with no further connections but to the final abyss, is where the surplus is collected and disposed of (that part of the surplus, at least, not abandoned, run over, or dead of disease or some other calamity). Shelter people do society's dirty work and call it "euthanasia," "putting down," or "putting to sleep," but mostly it is simply killing. A dose of sodium pentobarbital and in seconds the animals are gone. With these numbers they can find no hopeful alternative to a painless death caringly administered. They act and believe sincerely.

The dissonance is ethical, rational, and strategic or political. What does a life's intrinsic value mean in this situation? What does devotion to animal welfare mean? What happens to the credibility and potency of the welfarist message under these circumstances? And finally, how does it affect a guardian's motivation to take proper responsibility for animal procreation when welfare professionals daily dispose of the excess? (I repeat: Euthanasia as a caring response to untreatable suffering is *not* what usually happens at the shelter.) The inconsistencies run rampant, and compassionate intention does not resolve either them or the problems.

Contradiction reveals itself in other facets of shelter function. We say that dogs and cats are not disposable commodities and that no one should become their companion who is not prepared for lifetime commitment. Rather like deciding to become a parent, taking responsibility for another creature's life is not for the faint of heart or flaccidly loyal. We mean this. Yet the shelter has a door marked "receiving" and the majority of those who cross its threshold are guardians dropping off their animals. *Why?*, we ask. Well, they're moving, or don't have time for him anymore, or cannot tolerate the misbehavior, or it's the boyfriend, the allergies, the litter box, the children growing up, the new hairfree furniture. Diverse explanations, but all expressions of animal devaluation and unwillingness to commit. Staff who receive these animals are justifiably skeptical of claims for human nobility as a species.

But here we are again, saying one thing and doing something contrary. Animals are not disposable items; yet we will dispose of your animal. In fact, some take great pride in never turning an animal away. Shelter welfarists worry that not providing a refuge, however brief and terminable it might turn out, risks abuse, abandonment, suffering. Well-meaning this certainly is, illustrataing the rescuers' virtuous impulse. But do they, perversely and unconsciously, feed the demand for this service and negate the nondisposability message in the very act of caringly taking in? Does shelter compassion enable and facilitate behaviors toward animals that are precisely opposite its affirmed values? Does an irresponsible public attune to what animal authorities do rather than to what they say?

Another aspect of the shelter situation strikingly coheres with the essential welfare valuing of animal lives: the process and standards involved in counseling potential adopters of homeless animals. Yet here, where consistency finally emerges, a new kind of perverse effect appears.

Responsible shelters do not simply hand out animals to whoever wants one. One of the most common practical and public relations problems for shelters, in fact, particularly those that kill surplus, healthy animals, arises in the encounter between adopter and adoption counselor. The transaction frequently involves very different assumptions about what is or should be occurring, for ours is a consumerist society and many adopters believe they are engaged in a commercial transaction. At the mall they see, they want, they choose, they write their check and walk away with the goods, no questions asked. Not so at the shelter. The transaction composes an adoption—no more a purchase than occurs at a child-placing agency. The good of the adoptee is foremost and the counselor's task that of keeping it so while assessing for a suitable match.

Is the adopter prepared to give the time and make the commitment the animal needs? Does the breed and age fit his or her lifestyle? Any thoughts of declawing the cat or leaving the dog outside all the time? Is there a history of lost or run-over animals or ones casually relinquished? These are reasonable questions when one considers the adoptee a valued being rather than a commodity. Still, the questions can be personal, and adopters begin to feel interrogated and defensive. Additionally, the setting is rarely felicitous for the exchange. Shelters are notoriously crowded, noisy, and understaffed. Moreover, the encounter obviously requires tact and other human relations skills that staff who are first and foremost animal lovers may be short on. They are often young, poorly trained and paid, harried, and at a given moment, perhaps, still angry over yet another irresponsible guardian who has just dropped off his frightened former companion at receiving.

Clearly this represents a situation ripe for misunderstanding and conflict. As a result, adoption interviews sometimes fail to be consummated with a happy pairing. Occasionally, the counselor simply sees no way to responsibly place the chosen animal with the would-be adopter. The well-being of the particular animal or the likelihood of a successful match appears too precarious. Often, though, the adopter terminates the interchange, leaving in frustration or fury while flinging back toward the worker a shredded application and the accusation that he/she obviously prefers killing the animal to letting him go home with the one wanting him.

Here enters perversity in the form of the "law of unintended consequences." The animal sought, subject of the failed adoption encounter, has been saved entry into whatever potentially unsuitable domestic situation it was that concerned the shelter counselor. He is safe, at least until the fateful moment of overcrowding and "euthan- asia" selections: rescued from a possibly dangerous or otherwise undesirable situation but at the price of entry into another momentous gamble.

The wide sweep of the aforementioned law does not stop here. That person wanted an animal. Of all the dogs and cats in homes only about fifteen percent come from companion animal shelters. The rest are strays who "adopt" guardians or come from friends, breeders, pet stores, classified ads, or that universal individual with a litter in a box in front of the grocery store. Animals are not hard to come by! So, in lieu of an altered (one hopes) shelter animal, the seeker of an animal companion acquires one elsewhere that is probably unaltered, a procreative time bomb waiting to explode with its contribution to overpopulation and thus the shelter population. The danger averted for the originally sought shelter creature has simply been transferred to a different one rather than eliminated. The shelter animal may already be dead and the possibility of an educational relationship with the animal guardian equally inert. And now negative word-of-mouth from that person will discourage future shelter adoptions. Shelter behavior has coincided with shelter values, but with what effect, at what cost?

The companion animal welfare field has a problem that I characterize as a collection of behaviors and values deeply discrepant with one another. This results in impaired and self-defeating responses to the real problems in our culture's treatment of animals, diminished credibility as a voice for animals, and a role more minor than it should be as effective advocate for animals. If this description of the dynamics in receiving, "euthanasia," and adoption is close to the mark, what else could we expect?

~

I want to highlight several features of the shelter culture

rationale for traditional practice. Shelter staff recognize the abysmal cultural failure in relation to these animals, vigorously condemn it, and then set about cleaning up the mess consequent upon that failure. If the rectifying only involved sheltering, medical care, and placing lost or abandoned animals in new homes that would be one matter. But it goes so much farther, to killing the victims, and that surely moves the cleanup into a problematic realm. Death as a solution to problems of life is not just one other solution among many. Somehow the virtuous impulse has been coopted into the service of failure. Or so an outsider might think. As seen from within, the problems of homelessness and overpopulation are essentially irresolvable. Workers acknowledge that one must confront the causes resolutely while reminding society repeatedly of the problems, but for the most part those in the animal welfare and sheltering field have little or no real expectation of final success. This gloomy resignation suggests something of the underlying world view.

We are counseled to patience, for progress is being made (and it is). But do not expect too much too soon. The more immediate goal must be to reduce the size of the problem and the quota of suffering. In the meantime, the killing is unavoidable and welfarists must humanely shoulder the burden because if they do not, others inhumanely will. As one shelter worker put it, "I know the killing of society's surplus is wrong, but as of this moment I don't see any reasonable alternatives."

These are the common terms for ending the animals' lives: killing, euthanasia, putting down, putting to sleep. (One shelter's materials refer to it in certain cases as "culling with extreme prejudice" but I have only seen this usage once and find it so objectionable a term that I will say no more about it.) "Putting to sleep" denies the finality of events (like the "slumber room" at funeral homes or a cemetery called "Restland"), "putting down" neutralizes but obliquely describes, and "euthanasia" is usually a misnomer. I will only use the term here in the strict sense of its meaning: taking the life of one for whom no reasonable alternative exists in as painless and compassionate a fashion as possible and for the good and in the interests of the one whose life it is.

DISPOSABLE ANIMALS

Taking a life under circumstances that fail to meet these conditions is simply killing. While sometimes justifiable, it is not euthanasia.

Another feature of the rationale follows on one described above. In this case a tendency appears to discount the significance of adoption and euthanasia rates to shelter success. Adoptions lacking strict screening may lead to lower rates of euthanasia, the discounter says, but to what end? An animal soon returned to the shelter and much the worse for its experience? (High adoption and/or low euthanasia rates, according to this view, apparently must always conceal and rest upon craven compromise.) One aspires for an end to the killing, of course, but as an official of the Humane Society of the United States recently said (once again), "The alleviation of suffering is at the top of the list" of reasons for engaging in animal welfare work.

This alleviation-of-suffering rationale deserves scrutiny. The relation of the animal welfare worker to dogs and cats analogizes somewhat that of physician to patient (except that an unhappy patient can leave for a new physician). Both worker and doctor are in positions of authority and responsibility and can act in ways having serious consequences upon the life and health of their charges. Both will say they act only on behalf of the welfare of their "patients." But how will I react should my physician say that his first obligation is to alleviate my suffering? I might have a different set of priorities. His tradition adjures "primum non nocere"—first do no harm. Second, I am motivated to hope he/she might cure what afflicts me. And then third, I wish my suffering to be relieved. To place suffering at the head of the list, though, seems to partake of the fatalism already noted and to make some large and perilous assumptions, given their consequences. After all, hypothesized suffering (which it usually is) might not occur.

This raises an associated feature of the humane rationale, one central to its operation: Catastrophization. The rationale assumes that each compassionately killed animal has been spared not simply a less than ideally desirable life but an unspeakable fate. The Humane Society official mentioned above who pointed to the priority of alleviated suffering spoke also of "fates worse than death" for which "euthanasia" was the only feasible answer. Of "deaths worse than fate" we hear nothing. The certainty and clairvoyance with which humane defenders of the status quo apprehend the sufferings prevented by death is astonishing. Can they be sure that all, or even most, animals who might be turned away from a full shelter, with the owner or finder given suggestions for alternatives, would thereby be cast down into misery? Even if we somehow knew the odds pointed to that conclusion as a generalization, what about the specific individual animals implicated?

Something else goes on here, and I suggest it may be a piece of that cooptation of virtue mentioned earlier. These abundant animals are an inconvenience, and the traditional way of Western culture in handling such inconveniences is to shove them aside, lethally if necessary. This has been the fate of indigenous peoples and wildlife, just more violently inflicted, and here it arises again.

Yet another central feature of shelter rationale and function is the pervasive mentality of the rescuer. Rescuers require victims, and when victims appear there will be immense rescuing energy expended. Context, however, may suffer in the process. Whether the victims are companion animals, abused children, or substance abusers, rescuers notoriously miss the big picture and the long term. Thus arise the problems of unintended consequences, mismatched values and behaviors, and the perverse pride in "never turning an animal away" from even a full shelter. In years gone by children's group homes similarly fell prey to shortsighted rescuing while failing to see how it neglected parents and contributed to the emotional damage of many kids. Open door rescuing of unwanted animals and then saving them from questionable adopters, both under the specter of death, will have the unfortunate but foreseeable effect of enabling cultural malfeasance. For the pressure to change behavior and attitude dissipates when many of the living reasons for change are continually killed—efficiently, compassionately, invisibly, one-by-one.

In summary, the contemporary companion animal welfare movement gives a picture not altogether of failure but surely of good intention gone awry as killing continues as an acceptable response to animal overpopulation. The contradictions described raise an Orwellian aura around welfarists and shelters. They represent double messages, deeply so.

Psychotherapeutic theory says people typically respond in one of three ways to such messages. They may flee, an important matter relative to shelter "customers" considering the minuscule proportion of all companion animals who are adopted from shelters. Or they may go crazy, which in this situation figuratively is more a problem for shelter staffs than the public. Or they may choose a preferred message from the two offered and ignore the other. I suggest that this last alternative is the common one in animal shelters' contacts with the public and that the message taken is one of disposability. The credibility of a respect-promoting message cannot withstand constantly contrary behavior on the part of the sender, regardless of the humanitarian rationale and intent. When frustrated potential adopters exclaim that the shelter would rather kill the animal than let them have him, they voice genuine confusion. And not all of that can be explained away by the notion that they simply lack understanding or respect for animals.

Animal welfare occupies a quagmire of old ideas and inertia, of large-scale ethical and intellectual incongruities. To some extent this can be explained as the persistence of habits of thought and action that were once appropriate but which have grown anachronistic. Additionally, as Peter Singer has noted, animal welfare organizations have lost their early radicalism and evolved into the establishment. Both these observations help to account for a shelter conservatism that seems able to stare unblinkingly at bodies of evidence of failure while marching steadily onward in step with the same old music. Still, a deep curiosity remains. How are animal protectors of the most sincere and dedicated sort recruited, indoctrinated, and retained in so counterintuitive a response to animal needs and interests? We have seen the appeal to prevent suffering, but what of the larger intellectual and emotional context?

REFERENCES

Coleman, Sydney H. *Humane Society Leaders in America.* New York: American Humane Association, 1924.

Duvin, Ed. "In the Name of Mercy." *animalines*, Vol. 4, #11.

———. "Benign Neglect." *animalines*, Vol. 4, #12.

McRae, Roswell. *The Humane Movement.* New York: Columbia University Press, 1910.

Niven, Charles, D. *History of the Humane Movement.* London: Johnson Publications, 1967.

Schultz, William. *The Humane Movement in the United States: 1910-1922.* New York: Columbia University dissertation, 1924.

2

JUST KILLING

If vegetarians go to work at the slaughter house, what will we think? When "pro-life" adherents assume the burden of abortion, what then? Or animal liberationists writing protocols for more extensive animal experimentation? Efforts to reform from within, perhaps? Or the courageous effort to bring a gentler, more compassionate touch to condemned but presently unavoidable realms of behavior.

Such actions mystify because they do not match the advocates' expressed commitments. They suggest hidden motivations or extraneous influences. I contend that an animal welfarist who assumes the onus of killing healthy animals is just as morally and intellectually incoherent as the caricatures presented above. But they are not thoughtless or morally insensitive people, so I want to understand what they do and to present a plausible perspective on their moral reasoning.

One way of looking at this, which I will explore more fully in the next chapter, suggests that well-meaning people have somehow been captured unaware on behalf of intentions other than their own. I believe this partially explains the shelter role in our culture.

It brings to mind a scene from an old war movie, *Bridge on the River Kwai*. A captured British army engineer and his men are forced to build a militarily significant bridge for the enemy. As he is a competent man and dedicated to the highest standards of his craft, it becomes a very fine bridge indeed. But in order to stymie the enemy war efforts and aid their allies, those who have built the bridge must surreptitiously prepare to destroy their creation. In the scene, as I recollect it, the engineer resists the destruction (he is deeply absorbed with the bridge, his handiwork), until in a revelatory moment we see on his face the sudden illumination of who and where he is and who the enemy and what his overriding purpose is and must be. And down comes the bridge—right action reunited with right intention.

If shelter welfarists are unconsciously drafted into bridge-building for animals' adversaries, how is it accom- plished? I will examine aspects that focus on the ethical and psychological dimensions. In the next chapter I will discuss cooptation and cultural meanings. Naturally, these all combine and reinforce one another but for present purposes will be looked at separately.

As was discussed earlier, animal welfare and shelter organizations construe "euthanasia" of their animals as a lamentable but inescapable necessity. At some point in my effort to come to terms with this I began to understand it as a variant of a "just war" rationale. Traditional theorizing about the just war goes back at least to St. Augustine in the fifth century and arose from the effort to develop ways to justify something—war—which on the face of it constituted evil. The means of war are killing and destruction. Those who are morally sensitive but not pacifist want a way to evaluate when war can be justified as the least evil (or least good, as some have said) means to achieve important ends. In addition to the question of when war can justly be undertaken comes the question of how to conduct it rightly. Justice of a particular war then becomes a matter of rightness of occasion, procedures, and methods.

I do not suggest that we are at war with dogs and cats. Rather, just war principles provide an appropriate model for the effort to reason philosophically about killing healthy animals. We will find most of the same difficulties here, as we look at "euthanasia," that occur in the domain of war-making when it comes to weighing and measuring the criteria against one another. Still, it's a worthwhile exercise and provides a useful model to interpret welfarists' killing, even if not one they explicitly use.

The literature on just war theory is extensive and the enumeration of criteria reasonably consistent. As a preface let me refer to an observation common among its theorists. Nonmaleficence, the duty to cause no avoidable harm to others, constitutes a prima facie obligation of everyone always. Obligations, however, sometimes conflict such that not all can be satisfied in a given situation. To do no harm when one sees, for example, that innocent people need protection from aggressors may, except for pacifists, constitute a situation that justifies and even mandates war over peace. In the matter of present concern, respect for the lives of companion animals—respect for their right to live those lives— must sometimes, they say at the shelter, stand aside on behalf of more compelling obligations. How might these be established?

As I said at the outset, the objection here is not to *true* euthanasia. Any being—dog or cat, spouse or friend—for whom a caringly facilitated death seems the final respectful gift one can offer deserves access to euthanasia. So that is not our topic, but instead a theory for "just killing" of healthy and adoptable but homeless animals. This is so because one cannot assume that a healthy creature would likely consider death preferable to some easily imagined alternatives. In the absence of a euthanasia defense, can the deaths be justified on other grounds? The considerations I will examine are these: 1) the authority who chooses, 2) the cause, 3) last resort, 4) chances of success, 5) intention, 6) announcement of intention, 7) proportionality, and 8) conduct.

~

The authority who chooses: Justice of the problematic act begins with the criterion that the directive to kill issues from a legitimate and competent authority. And since authority in the shelter setting lacks the power to compel the unwilling to carry out the directive, we assume that he who kills affirms authority's judgment. Since killing homeless animals has been accepted practice in the United States for well over a century, and since millions of donors knowingly contribute to shelters that kill, and public animal control departments perform and contract to have performed such killing, and managers of shelters create job descriptions requiring killing as a routine duty—given all of this, the criterion of authority's legitimacy appears satisfied. Authority's competence, however, may be a different matter, one that I will discuss below. For now I say only that competence implies that all the criteria for just killing have been carefully considered and adequately satisfied. The burden of responsibility lies heavily upon any who affirm or accede to the practice, and one may wonder about the depth, clarity, and assiduousness brought to this task by many who exercise authority over life and death.

Why, for example, has there not been more serious debate within the field? The response to Duvin, remember, was emotional and personalized and only begged the central question he raised. Similarly, the responses I received from opponents of our renunciation of killing were singularly vitriolic and pejoratively labeling and continued begging the question. So well defended and insular a system rarely reflects thoroughly on its premises or the nonobvious effects of its actions, and to that extent its competence is compromised.

The cause: A second consideration arises around the question of "just cause." Do the values sought in killing the animal supersede those implicit in the duty not to harm? Substantiation of just killing will depend crucially on the answer to this. The typical response appeals to the alleviation or prevention of suffering (life-saving being traditionally and notoriously short-shrifted). To succeed, this appeal must identify real suffering or accurately predict that "fates worse than death" await unkilled homeless (and potentially homeless) animals. I know from experience the certainty of this conviction among those involved, having seen people weep in dreadful anticipation of what not being killed would entail for the animals. The validation of a just killing demands that this certainty be well founded.

We will discuss below in greater detail the moral and intellectual incoherence of the welfarist rationale. It arises here, for instance, in the question of whose cause the killing serves.

Are there some not-so-just causes supported by this deadly disposition? Community convenience and evasion of individual responsibility are possibilities. Killing evident victims to save them from further victimization might suffice as an emergency measure, but as an institutionalized policy this displays the same futile syndrome as other endeavors where symptoms rather than causes are the focus. Further, does shelter killing apply a group solution to individual problems? It seems to in that surely no one has the prescience to know that all the animals killed would otherwise have suffered grievously, yet all are dead.

To illustrate the significance of this we can consider the following thought experiment: A hundred of us are in a room and suddenly and authoritatively we are informed from above that in a short while 75 will be cast into vast suffering from which each would beg release through euthanasia. Unfortunately, we cannot know which 75. Either all 100 or none will be euthanized, and we must decide which it will be now! How many ask for the needle? How many wish to take their chances?

Last resort: If we granted that the cause were a just one (even though mired in questionable assumptions), we must still inquire about alternative means of achieving the goal of preventing and alleviating suffering. Killing, after all, represents a decidedly radical approach to problem-solving and its finality ought to stir some powerful creative energies.

If you visit someone living in a retirement community, you eventually hear it referred to with solemn humor as "God's waiting room." Shelter culture, minus the theological aspirations, conceives itself similarly as a last hope and penultimate stop. A fortunate minority of incoming creatures find homes, but the rest have nowhere left to go. And since "euthanizing" shelters are committed never to turn an animal away, there eternally are more with nowhere left. With this commitment, added to limited space and limited homes— no available niche in either nature or culture—killing seems the last resort, lamentable but unavoidable. Shelter staff are sure of this.

Two objections arise to the "last resort" hypothesis. The first is tactical: How can we deal most effectively with a chronic problem—through prevention or treatment? The same question permeates discussions in medicine, mental health, criminology, and social dysfunction in general. Typically, prevention receives major doses of lip service while resources flow into remediative efforts, even when they produce little more effect than running-in-place. What else can we expect given daily exposure to battered casualties and limited financial and compassionate resources?

Yet the problem is chiefly one of guardian responsibility and numbers, and the solutions are not buried in obscurity. Routine sterilization, preferably on pre-pubescent animals, will relieve a large part of it. In areas where assiduous public information campaigns or controversy have forced the issue into public awareness, you generally see dramatic declines in shelter intake figures. But not yet enough and to the shame of many shelters little change in their adoption practices and numbers.

So two next-to-last resorts suggest themselves. First, shelters might get out of the rut of waiting patiently for customers to come to them and instead develop more aggressive adoption strategies. After all, their pet "market share" is only around 15% so ample room exists for expansion through such means as outreach, advertising, and public commentary on the true nature and ramifications of competing sources of animals. Since they kill the surplus they have a fatefully significant obligation to fill that room with aspiring shelter alumni.

Second, and more controversial, companion animal welfarists might declare themselves "conscientious objectors" to the killing. They could declare "peace," let the streets fill with dogs and cats if need be, and become noisy, assertive, and unrelenting in confronting people with the moral dimensions and demands of the human-companion animal relationship. "We will no longer kill your mistakes and the casualties of your irresponsibility," they could say, "but we will help in every other way imaginable to stop the problem before it is born and to find non-lethal solutions afterwards." This option accepts the possibility of short-term increases in suffering on behalf of the long-term good of obviated killing and the preservation and enhancement of animal lives.

In a metaphorical "just war" against overpopulation and killing the surplus, these would be soldiers in the battle for moral responsibility on the part of those who would be companions to animals. It is unconscionable for so much death to continue resulting from so preventable a problem.

The other objection to "last resort" as a killing defense concerns those animals arriving at the shelter not as strays, who are the truly homeless, but in the company of their companions. Hapless creatures in a morally odd situation, disposables of commoditized existences, they represent a potent indictment on the state of our relations with animals. I implied above that shelter killing of surplus animals may reduce the urgency of prevention: "disappeared" beings may be out of mind as well as sight. Now I suggest that a relatively casual open door policy at the shelter may have similarly self-defeating results. To speak of lifetime commitment and the preciousness of all life on one hand, while taking in (when there is no room to keep them) and killing with the other contradicts oneself. Another next-to-last resort then would 1) raise the threshold in the receiving department, 2) discourage drop-offs while offering guardians alternatives to deserting the animal to an uncertain fate, and 3) facilitate guardian-arranged adoptions in lieu of sheltering. Abandonment of these animals must be stigmatized, reluctant but unavoidable animal relinquishments assisted, and shelter behavior line up better with shelter values.

Chances of success: Another criterion in the justification of killing rests in the notion of a reasonable hope of success. Success means many things, takes different forms. Were we discussing war it could include victory (but not necessarily) along with accomplishment of other goals and affirmation of other values. Sometimes the latter are vital even when chances of victory appear remote, as in defense of cherished ideals and attachments against overwhelming odds. In the matter at hand, successful prevention of hypothesized suffering is guaranteed: sodium pentobarbitol is strong stuff and ends suffering decisively, along with all other potential experiencing. But it's a victory of great cost and not only for the dead animal.

The power of animal welfare values, the cogency of our

ideas, and the influence of our voice weaken with each additional corpse. Furthermore, jumbled priorities—placing relief from suffering over saving a life—sorely diminishes momentum. Even if such relief were adequate as a temporary measure, how can we accept it as a permanent answer? When we assuage suffering while allowing a progressive but preventable malady to continue carrying victims toward oblivion, we disappoint the deepest need.

Intention: A fifth criterion of justness concerns intention, the subjective dimension of just cause. It asks about motivation and suggests that bad or confused intention on behalf of a good cause mars the effort. The question addresses individually everyone involved in the killing and collectively the entire organizational field.

I will not challenge the historical affirmation of compassionate intent. The practice arose at a time when black humans were owned by white humans, when evolutionary biology was only incipient, and the human/animal differentiation vastly overstated (as it com- monly still is). The prospects for health, contentment, and respectful treatment for homeless animals were mostly grim at that time, and organized action for animal welfare only beginning. But much has changed, not the least of which involves the growth of a fairly well-fed and articulate welfare movement which must ask itself if the continuation of killing does not perpetuate an archaic way of thinking that in the end undermines good intention. History provides many examples of the negative effects arising from meliorative intention—from medicinal bleed- ing and purging to lobotomy and thalidomide. To consider the relief of suffering as a highest purpose seems flawed by the putting of second things first and first things second.

Announcement of intention: This criterion requires publicizing what lies behind the decision and rationale. And it reflects the seriousness of the action. Although the privacy of killing facilitates the public's avoidance of reality, and thorough analysis of alternative routes has been insufficient, I will not quibble that shelter killing has not been announced—even if under the usually misplaced, euphemistic epithet "euthanasia."

Proportionality: The seventh criterion requires that the costs of killing are proportional to the values sought. More simply, greater overall good than harm will come about.

If one believes that the only alternative to death for an animal is a life of endless, unrecompensed suffering, then a swift and painless end will be a fitting gift. But the questions raised earlier reflect on the conventional wisdom in this realm. Here we join the discussion of euthanasia's appropriateness for humans: how much suffering and what life quality coalesce around a right decision for euthanasia? These are considerations of the most serious sort, and a strict ethic will demand that decisions be made on individual rather than collective grounds. For example, the class "homeless animals" will not do for it is not a class that either suffers or dies. To systematically kill with no end in sight based on a presumption that alternatives are uniformly and predictably unthinkable resounds with blinkered and calcified thinking.

Conduct: The eighth and final criterion from just war tradition relates to just conduct. But here the practice of war faces a more complex issue than ours. Reputable animal care organizations invest a great deal of energy and resources in proper training, equipping, and support of personnel who do the killing. Pride is voiced only about deaths that are carefully, painlessly, and stresslessly administered. In short, technical conduct in these organizations is admirable.

But the tradition of just conduct also addresses the issue of discrimination in the application of force: how much of what kinds against whom, with a presumption of immunity for noncombatants. The questions raised above about a group-based solution to individual problems and the need to sharply assess many situations are equally applicable here. Is a killing force imposed on animals who do not require it, who are not suffering, and who might have other alternatives?

Incoherent Rationalization

We have reviewed the eight criteria: the authority who chooses, the cause, last resort, chances of success, intention, announcement of intention, proportionality, and con-

47

duct. Each consideration applied to the possibility of justly killing healthy animals stands on weak footing.

Intention labors under the strain of inverted priorities and euphemism. Just conduct fails on the grounds of non-discrimination—animals are killed for membership in a category rather than after individual assessment of suffering that cannot be relieved. (If that's said to be unrealistic because of the numbers, we must ask whose discomfort these deaths ease.)

Proportionality suffers from the same weakness as well as another—unintentionally prolonging the problems of animal overpopulation and disposability through their antiseptic removal by those wearing the robes of animal welfare. Strenuous effort to rescue the victims here leads to the irony of enabling further victimization. The criterion of a reasonable hope of success teeters under the same burden.

The three remaining considerations—last resort, just cause, and competent authority—point most clearly to the intellectual and moral incoherence I mentioned at the beginning. By incoherent I mean disjointed, inconsistent, contradictory. These rationales for killing will not hold together.

To illustrate this I will look at several articles from the literature on "euthanasia" and the kill—no-kill debate. Most of these sources came through a local public library's reference department, acquired by them from the Humane Society of the United States in response to a request for information on these subjects. Since HSUS supports shelter "euthanasia," we must assume they consider these representative and effective statements on its behalf, particularly since one appeared in *Shelter Sense* which is an HSUS publication. I will summarize three articles and reserve comment until the end.

The first, by Rhonda Donald, is called "The No-Kill Controversy." She begins by telling us that "The task of the shelter that euthanizes animals is to educate this person [one who surrenders his animal with the hope she will be adopted] on why euthanasia is a reality and a necessity." She continues: "The conflict between 'kill' and 'no-kill' philosophies really boils down to who accepts the responsibility for having to destroy animals." Some no-kill facilities are well run and some not, but the real issue is not that but philosophy. Referring to a shelter director speaking about no-kills, she says "he believes that their tactics undermine educational efforts. 'We go into schools and talk about being a responsible pet owner,' he says. 'But all the kids can see is that we kill animals. The public doesn't want to accept the reality, so the no-kill shelters become the good guys.'"

In addition to the philosophical difference, no-kills are "forced to limit their services." Thus, the Humane Society of Charlotte must use a waiting list for owner releases and, according to its director, "most people are willing to wait." But that was not good enough for Phyllis Wright, former HSUS Vice President for companion animals: "It's the ones who aren't willing to wait that concern [her]." Similarly, another shelter director "believes that no-kill shelters provide an out for the public to dump animals. No-kills say, 'bring 'em here; we won't kill 'em.' It's a dumping ground."

Besides philosophy and service limitation, the final objection to no-kills concerns the future of unkilled animals. "I don't worry about one of those animals who were put to sleep," said Wright. "I worry a great deal about dogs and cats who have to spend their lives shut in small cages or runs or left chained to the back porch day-in and day-out without affection or companionship. Being half-alive is more cruel than being dead." The solution to the conflicts between kill and no-kill adherents? "The key to getting people to understand the need for euthanasia is education combined with a strong spay/neuter program."

"The Truth About 'No kill' Animal Shelters" is a 1987 article written by Leon Nielsen, Executive Director of the Wisconsin Humane Society. An advocate for "full service" humane societies, he laments the public relations difficulties of countering the no-kill sentiment, which he believes to be based on ignorance of the facts. To correct this, he resorts to math. In 1986 his facility "euthanized" 18,000 dogs and cats. Since it could only hold 350 at a time, not killing would have meant building a new shelter more than 50 times its size. Very expensive, of course, not to mention the next year when another 18,000 capacity facility would be needed, and the next ad infinitum, seemingly with only natural mortality ebbing the tide.

On the shoulders of these mathematical certainties stand other reinforcing convictions. No-kill shelters "are not obligated morally, contractually or otherwise, to accept any animal brought to their facility. While a bona fide humane society, on the basis of its charter, is obligated to accept all animals." From this belief follow others which he embraces with equal adamancy: no-kills will accept only the most adoptable animals; when they err and take some that turn out unadoptable they will "eventually take these animals secretly to a humane society or veterinarian to have them euthanized"; they will redefine adoptability such that any animal they kill or have killed is defined as unadoptable; and they will end up warehousing animals in unhealthy, inhumane circumstances where they will suffer grievously until rescued and "euthanized" by welfarists with the courage to face necessity.

The final voice on these questions comes from the Executive Director of the Michigan Humane Society, an organization that, he tells us, "euthanizes" almost 80% of the animals passing through it. Inevitably (apparently), no-kills "cause profound suffering in the name of humaneness." Animals are warehoused for years often in unhealthy physical conditions and always emotionally unhealthy ones. Paradoxically, he says they also only accept the most adoptable animals. Alternatively, "The MHS never closes its doors to any animal in need. We believe that we as a progressive animal protection organization have a responsibility to all animals who find themselves in need, not just the young ones, the cute ones or the ones we have room for today. We will occasionally ask individuals if they can bring their animals back in a few days, and if they cannot, we accept the animal into our care without question or exception." As with Mr. Nielsen above, he has numbers. Were MHS a no-kill shelter it would have to build housing for 100,000 animals within three years. Finally, he references a leader in another humane society in order to reiterate a common claim against no-kill shelters: "these shelters aren't really 'no-kill' shelters. They are 'you-kill' shelters meaning that their clean hands and pure hearts exist at the expense of other shelters like the MHS which accept the animals they will not." The battle against companion animal overpopulation "is best waged by facing reality and accepting responsibility for all unfortunate animals in need."

Discussion

Let me say again that I made this excursion into pro-"euthanasia" literature in order to illustrate its failure, due to incoherence, to satisfy the demand of "just killing" that it be determined by competent authorities as a last resort action for a just cause.

What have we seen? First, these traditional shelter welfarists beg the most serious questions: Is it right and is it effective (regarding the long-term and long-standing problems of animal overpopulation, disposability, and putative suffering) to kill these animals? Ms. Donald says repeatedly that philosophy underlies the difference between kill and no-kill but never addresses this fundamental ethical and pragmatic issue. Rather, she and the others ignore it and assume, without defending, an affirmative answer. They propound reality and necessity as self-evident propositions before which the long-suffering but responsible animal welfarist must bow.

Having accepted without evident examination this burden of necessity, they also exclude the possibility of acceptable alternatives to killing. The usual "fates worse than death" hover ubiquitously around the shelter-as-refuge foreground while a monolithic view of no-kill shelter irresponsibility provides the background for this closed gestalt. Then there are numbers, ironically provided by shelter directors with dramatic fatality ratios as well as total body counts. It would seem that neither of their organizations manages to return strays to their companions or to arrange adoptions after the initial holding period since their scenarios seem to describe ceaseless entry with no ambulatory exits.

Leaving aside the statistical confusion, this elevated concern with entry over exit provides another illustration of incoherence. Recall that no-kills are accused of limiting their services, of not being "full service" shelters—a strange term in this context since the service fullness consists in never turning an animal away and killing the overflow. Taking great, if perverse, pride in ever-open arms, these shelters see themselves as places of animal salvation, no matter that the salvation can be lethal. This will of course be denied, but how else to explain the traditionally unimaginative approach to adoption promotion and other initiatives despite the stagnant adoption levels and high mortality numbers year after year?

To compound the exclusion of alternatives, add a dose of self-righteousness. No-kills (a.k.a. you-kills) only pass the buck to more responsible shelters willing to bear that burden of assumed necessity. Since one can always resign a job requiring "euthanasia," and contracts and charters can be ended or changed, this is a strange charge. If the killing is wrong they ought not do it; if it is right they ought not complain about it, at least not lay their complaints before those who have conscientiously chosen a different way of committing to animal well-being.

Echoing the Catholic sociologist Gordon Zahn on war, a follower of the no-kill way might sound like this: "I, as a pacifist, would prefer risking the evils we might have to endure as a result of too rigid an exclusion of war to the evils we would certainly be called upon to commit as the result of too easy an acceptance of actions deemed 'necessary' by some military leader, thereby meeting the test of the 'just' war." Knowing the history of systematized forms of killing in general and endless companion animal killing in particular, one shuns a non-killing alternative at some moral risk.

The question cannot be avoided. If you are killing 80% of the animals coming your way while standing immovably on the continued necessity and compassion of that route, are you more a part of the problem than of a solution? If the suggested treatment for your disease had a mortality rate of 80%, would you rush out to assure that your insurance covered it, or instead to find an alternative treatment? Further, with the corpses still stacked high after decades of the killing treatment, who exactly receives the benefits of the "full service" shelter?

I must speak to the shelter director's charge that no-kill shelters are "dumping grounds" in that they offer non-lethal placement for guardian-released animals. This is a peculiar indictment and one difficult not to construe as a form of projection. My arguments against "eutha- nasia" are moral and pragmatic. These rest largely on the observation that shelters contradict themselves when they say, at one moment, companion animals deserve relationships of utmost commitment and deep respect for the intrinsic value of their lives, and at the next, that a "full service" shelter will turn none away even if the place is full and a newcomer's admission equals death for another. Surely here lies the true dumping ground. And the contradiction costs more than meets the eye for it not only enshrouds the dumping but it perpetuates the disposability syndrome as well. It also applies a patina of rectitude, for after all, animal lovers are in charge.

Only killing done to relieve irremediable suffering will meet the standard of last resort for a just cause. Richard Niebuhr, the theologian, once referred to life as "a crucial affair." A wonderful piece of understatement pointing to life's unending mystery and depth. Debate about euthanasia of humans reveals, among other things, a certain appreciation of this. Killing surely must be our last resort, and its prevention our just cause.

Conclusion

Belief in "euthanasia" of companion animals gives the appearance of anachronistic dogma. It begs, when it should explore, questions about the value of all life, it systematically avoids evidence of failure, excludes alternative views and attacks those who broach them, and in a most thoroughgoing way it confabulates as virtue and necessity routine killing as antidote for suffering. The question that ended the first chapter—how are animal welfarists sustained in this business?—has a partial answer now. A doctrine for the "just killing" of healthy companion animals involves a range of weighty considerations. But rather than give them their due, companion animal welfarism takes a more one-dimensional outlook: suffering abatement through, of necessity, "euthanasia." Killing causes the perpetrator exceeding pain, but the paradigm rationalizes it and alleviates his own resultant suffering. Intellectually at least. But what of the powerful emotions involved?

The paradigm attempts to resolve, or conceal, contradictions in the welfarist stance between actions and values, intentions and results. But even one committed to the necessity of "euthanasia" will acknowledge contradiction between valuing and killing animals. And outside the shelter lies the mirror image contradiction: a public that is often suspicious of or downright negative toward the killing while themselves being responsible for most of the problems that are said to necessitate it. This situation has an interesting and paradoxical effect on shelter workers. On one hand it results in a sense of stigmatization and occasional social discomfort. They are the "execu- tioners," the misunderstood doers of the dirty work. On the other hand it helps evade the fatal inconsistencies in the welfare mystification, for it foments a righteous anger (which is altogether appropriate in regard to public irresponsibility, abuse and neglect of companion animals). But the next step is logically unsound even if consoling: the public becomes the source of "euthanasia" as the necessary response. There are obvious psychological benefits in transferring responsibility for what no one likes doing onto outsiders. And the anger can be emotionally purifying and strengthening and can be channeled into sincere action to reduce animal births and increase human responsibility. All these together—blame, anger, non-lethal attacks on the problems—help to alleviate the moral and emotional stresses of "euthanasia."

They also foster insularity, which has its own benefits in dealing with the emotions of this situation. "Us" against "them" can be powerful medicine, particularly when it helps build group solidarity. Shelter workers form a tightly knit community, and for many good reasons. Passionately involved with animals and committed to their welfare, distinguished by the willingness and the courage to express devotion through killing, internally battered by the moral ambiguity of this, self-perceived as safe havens for the animals in an indifferent, often hostile world—these are ties that bind and protect and to some extent heal.

Shelter workers naturally adopt normal defense mechanisms in the face of pain and contradiction. Denial, avoidance, projection, rationalization, and so on serve here as well as elsewhere and usually with more intense need. But I have come to believe that what chiefly makes it possible for them to continue is the power of their community. That community is extremist in commitment and action and defined by a collective sense of compassion, necessity, and rectitude. It is not understood and perhaps not understandable (they feel) by the larger community, and shares a certain specialness from all this. It is a community with a purpose: to protect and care and sometimes to "mercifully" kill. Mercy's close associate, however, is justice, and both seem to be lacking in this culture which mostly just wants someone to dispose of these animals.

REFERENCES

Arluke, Arnold. "Coping With Euthanasia: A Case Study of Shelter Culture." *JAVMA*, Vol. 198, #7, pp. 1176-1180.

Donald, Rhonda Lucas. "The No-Kill Controversy." *Shelter Sense*, September 1991, pp. 3-6.

Elshtain, Jean Bethke (ed.). *Just War Theory.* Washington Square: New York University Press, 1992.

Miller, Richard. *Interpretations of Conflict.* Chicago: University of Chicago Press, 1991.

Nielsen, Leon. "The Truth About 'No-Kill' Animal Shelters." *Animal Talk*, Vol. 1, #2, Summer 1987.

Owens, C., R. Davis, & B. Smith. "The Psychology of Euthanizing Animals: The Emotional Components." *INT. J. STUD. ANI.*, 2(1) 1981, pp. 19-26.

Shannon, Thomas A. (ed.). *War or Peace.* Maryknoll, N.Y.: Orbis Books, 1980.

Tiscornia, Gary. "Letter From the Executive Director." Michigan Humane Society Newsletter (n.d.).

Wright, Phyllis. "Why We Must Euthanize." *Humane Society News*, Summer 1978.

3

CULTURE, COOPTATION, AND DISPOSABILITY

If we want to understand how so morally odd a response to homeless companion animal problems has arisen and maintained itself, we cannot stop with shelter practice and rationale. That would be neither fair nor complete. Notwithstanding the critique presented here, the status of animals in our society depends critically on renewed and invigorated engagement by those in (and brought in) to the field of animal welfare—people with deep belief in the rights of animals to genuine welfare. Hope for such renewal and engagement is precisely the motivation for making the critique.

So we must go farther and look at the context that permits and encourages the syndrome. Specifically, what cultural patterns foster animal devaluation, and how are animal protectors drafted into the mission of killing its victims.

Beginning with the culture, we see a dominant constellation of values, aspirations, and activities that can be referred to collectively as "commodification." This orientation is composed of particular relations to material goods and consumption, work and uses of time, and a public discourse dominated by economic forces and their hirelings in the advertising industry. Indeed, commodification's power carries it well beyond the economic realm into relations among humans, with nature, with companion animals—relations in each case depleted of responsiveness and higher meanings and reduced to calculations of use and gain.

An example of a type common in our time: Early this

year ('96) the *Seattle Times* Sunday magazine reported on Port Gamble, "A Living Museum." Port Gamble is a small community on the Kitsap Peninsula about an hour by ferry and car northwest of Seattle. An old-fashioned company town, it was 142 years old when the log mill that sustained it all that time was closed late last year. Many of the workers were second or third generation at the mill, and virtually all had lived in company houses in the town for many years.

Distinguished by New England-style Victorian architecture, its history, and community cohesion, Port Gamble charms and attracts. I have walked its few streets and looked out over the bay, and while its participation in the diminishment of surrounding forests leaves me cold, I still felt the integrity, the connectedness of and within the place, and was warmed by that. Although the specific sources of the mill's and consequently the community's demise were not made clear by the company, to increase profitability surely was the decisive factor. "Whatever we do at Port Gamble," said the company president, "will be market-driven."

Under the circumstances that sentiment resoundingly strikes a dissonant chord. It sounds coarse and morally abdicative—the sort of thing whose truth the president might have been expected to disguise out of embarrassment. Yet he showed no discomfort. After all, it's just business, and the bottom line has no room on it for squeamish sentimentality.

Another example: For thirty-one years, until two months ago, New York's Simon & Schuster owned H.M. Gousha Co., a map-making business with 80 employees in a small Central Texas town called, ironically, Comfort. One morning in April, employees arrived for work and were greeted by security guards and locks and were denied entry. It seems that Simon & Schuster had sold Gousha to Rand McNally, which bought it in order to close it down. They did not want the company, but it was competition. Schuster sold out because "[Gousha] did not fit into its 'global' strategy." In this manner another community becomes sacrificial fodder for commodity-oriented culture, an acceptable casualty for the sake of business.

These examples demonstrate commodification's valuing

of communities of people. We all know how it similarly values individuals who for one reason or another become expendable. Or mere nature.

In 1913 the Sierra Nevadas' Hetch Hetchy Valley, described by some as a smaller replica of the Yosemite Valley, sublime in its beauty, became a reservoir, dammed and inundated to slake San Franciscans' thirst for moisture and money. Roderick Nash quotes Gifford Pinchot, the original apostle of "wise use," as saying that wilderness preservation was an appealing thing "if nothing else were at stake." He pointed out that "the fundamental principle of the whole conservation policy is that of use, to take every part of the land and its resources and put it to that use in which it will serve the most people." Fifty years later an identical fate with the same motivations befell Glen Canyon on the Colorado River north of Grand Canyon. Look at Eliot Porter's pictures in *The Place No One Knew*, feel the former beauty of it all, stand as I have on the dam looking northeastward, and think about commodification, loss, and disposability.

These things point to an overgrown and cannibalizing culture of consumption and use, one that promotes a servant relationship to commodity values as the summit of human aspiration while impoverishing others.

What chance have companion animals? We know that by noon today, and again by midnight, and again tomorrow, and the day after and on and on, the animal commodifiers without peer—those in the food industry—will slay as many creatures as animal welfare does in a year. A painful and revealing story itself, but few people claim an affectionate relation with those sad creatures (not that that should matter). Yet they do with dogs and cats, while still immersed in a commodity orientation. Is a world mesmerized by consumerism (and habituated to the byproducts of its omnivorous appetites) likely to be one where killing certain of its casual excesses would find an acceptable home?

Commodification, of course, does not move across the land in silence. Its voice is advertising, currently an almost $200 billion per year industry in the United States alone. While we may question the buyers and sellers of advertising on grounds of taste and values, one doubts they are so imprudent as to throw this kind of money around to no effect. It must accomplish sponsors' purposes. The pandering of illusions, a matter of dubious means in pursuit of questionable ends, particularly when aimed at children, seems an unworthy endeavor. But it is simply normal activity in commodity culture.

What may be most powerful in terms of cultural dominance is the constancy and ubiquity of advertising's message. Thousands upon thousands of businesses and products beseech incessantly through all manner of aural and visual media, but all shout the same monotonous song. A single theme envelops our world: If you awake to a radio and drift off to the evening news the first and last words of your day most likely repeat it; morning television and newspaper hum along; radio during the commute, and billboards; contents of your mail and unwanted telephone solicitations; evening television; magazines; school districts putting it on the sides of their buses to generate revenue—"ad" nauseam. The message: "BUY!" A thousand tongues, a single idiom.

If a religious or political message hounded us so, and we could not protect our children from it, we would find it intolerable. As theme music for daily activity, as leitmotif for life stories and cultural narrative, the message fosters commodity as ultimate organizing principle.

The philosopher John Rodman speculated about cultural patterns "that the same basic principles are manifested in quite diverse forms—e.g., in damming a wild river and repressing an animal instinct (whether human or nonhuman), in clear-cutting a forest and bombing a city, in Dachau and a university research laboratory, in censoring an idea, liquidating a religious or racial group, and exterminating a species of flora or fauna." These principles must be recognized and spoken aloud, for they are destructive to forest communities and human ones, companion animals and more. And we see in this also a second feature of cultural devaluations—the linkage of commodification with aggression and violence.

The history of European encroachment into the Western Hemisphere, as we know, began with both these features predominant: commodification and aggression, both rooted in devaluation of other being. David Stannard's 1992 book on that early encounter aptly named its reality: *American Holocaust*. Within only a generation or two the Americas experienced a demographic collapse of roughly 95% of their indigenous population, which before the Conquest may have been over one hundred million people. In the future United States they were considered "surplus populations," and for many Europeans their declining numbers merely reflected a divine cleansing preparatory to a more fruitful occupation of the land. The historian Lewis Hanke extends the appraisal, observing that "the idea of the unfitness of natives and their inferiority to Europeans appeared in whatever far corners of the world Europeans reached." Another said of the Spanish Conquest, "It would become the metamorphosis of man into a thing, passing through a first metamorphosis of man into a beast...which would climax in the transformation of man into a commodity."

In short, our history and culture run deep with hierarchies in which self-affirmed superiors dominate others. We can think of slavery (millions kidnapped and delivered into bondage, their continent colonized and partitioned), the treatment of women, industrialism's exploitation of children (first as workers, now as consumers), abuses of nature, extinctions, and we see those "same basic principles." As Elie Wiesel said of the more recent Holocaust, it "did not arise in a void but had its roots deep in a tradition that prophesied it, prepared for it, and brought it to maturity." One of the tradition's preeminent characteristics, I believe, is this aggressive devaluing, the transformation of the other into a thing ultimately emptied of all but manipulated worth. We ourselves are not exempt, and even less so, certainly, the animals.

Humans abuse and neglect their animal companions routinely. Others who care deeply for their fellow creatures want to help and may in their ways of doing it end up exacerbating the problem. Their chosen and often reiterated mission is to relieve suffering, to protect animals from "fates worse than death," and to accomplish this, they kill. Does their induction into this mission amount in some large measure to cooptation of a virtuous impulse?

Cooptation occurs when one is induced to promote or

tolerate aims other than his own. It can happen unconsciously, but when conscious will be neutralized in some way, as in rationalization or minimization. It is not compelled; the coopted accepts his role, sometimes enthusiastically. It helps when means and ends and their conceptual linkages are paradoxical, ambiguous, or incoherent. When the coopted believes himself to serve a transcendent good and focuses with passionate and narrow vision upon that good, he can endure considerable inconsistency, sustained by convictions that seem to reconcile incompatible values and strategies.

Contracts for animal "care and control" between public bodies and animal welfare organizations usually contain reference to the importance of keeping animals from becoming public nuisances. Who can argue with the need to control nuisances, of whatever species or type? In the case of dogs and cats on the loose, concerns about danger to others and disease and death for them are certainly legitimate. Other cases, though, are problematic. Guardians who want legitimized, convenient, and more or less guilt-free disposability of their animals describes one, and killing the victims of others' nonfeasance is another.

To alleviate suffering: This is the virtuous impulse. It finds and relieves hurting creatures daily. It offers euthanasia as a caring gift for the good of the recipient. The giver deserves respect in this situation.

But supporters of this kind of giving sometimes lack discrimination. When asked to refuse to kill until the suffering actually arrives or seems unavoidable or irremediable, uncensored first responses question where all the animals will go, not how they suffer. For clearly, not all those targeted are suffering. If only one out of three or four of the dead (an impressionistic best guess) are in truth euthanized (in the strict sense of the word), what are we doing and for whom?

Much of the problem here derives from continued treatment of the "open door" as necessity and virtue. I deny the indiscriminate necessity and therefore the virtue of such practice. And I believe that the heart of animal welfare's cooptation lies in its deathgrip-like embrace of that presumed necessity. Further, the practice self-perpetuates as it legiti-

CULTURE, COOPTATION, AND DISPOSABILITY

mizes and facilitates animal disposability.

Cooptation has a purpose, and disposability names it. Legions of people want to have "pets" at will, to behave responsibly or not toward those animals as it pleases them, to turn them out or to shelters at will, to not feel morally chastened for dereliction, to have streets cleansed of dead or wandering strays. Wanting to dispose of both their animal and the moral onus for his or her fate, where better to go than to animal protectors? Inadvertently these caring people end up sanctioning and enabling that which they abhor. Alleviating the suffering of some through euthanasia, they are convinced that that is what they always do.

~

I have wanted in the above to illustrate the remorseless domination of Western culture's major projects and values by the commodity orientation toward being. In its broad outlines nothing in this portrayal should surprise us. But I fear that animal welfare's repeated invocation of the problem of "disposable animals within a disposable culture" has lost much of its reality, its sting, and has fallen into cliche.

More than half the households in this country include companion animals. Their guardians are relentlessly discouraged from making binding commitments. They are indoctrinated with what has been called "commodity fetishism," which requires a preoccupation with obtaining things (and animals) but not attaching so much that trading-in for the newest models would be delayed. The message is powerful, and shelter workers daily deal with its ramifications for dogs and cats.

But shelter culture too exists within the ceaseless din and under the dismal shadow of this message. At the shelter these issues and the burden of other lives translate from abstraction into physical presence. There we find aspects of foster and group homes, retail establishments, ICU's, hospice, and death camp. At its best the shelter provides a voice and vital transitional care for homeless animals: room and board, medical and surgical treatment, sterilization, education, advocacy, training, and adoption to homes offering full membership in the family. But one assumes a large and problematic burden, in moving beyond that, when he chooses to act on behalf of another in matters of life and death—whether a physician contemplating euthanasia for a mortally ill patient or a shelter worker prepared to kill a healthy animal to protect her from potential suffering.

We need more clarity about this matter of disposability as an evil and of the proper response to it. Clearly, not all disposing is wrong; each of us disposes of everything from old clothes to soft drink containers every day and mostly without moral qualm. But many add additional steps to the process: They ask if they really need the item before they acquire it (knowing it will eventually require disposition); they consider whether they can obtain it with minimal throwaway packaging, and think about what parts can be recycled or reused. In short, they make acquisition and disposition matters of concern, and not because of a sense of obligation to aluminum or cardboard, but out of commitment and gratitude to Earth, the community of life. This ultimate commitment gives moral weight to these smaller matters along the way; it makes disposability an issue it would not be without such commitment.

Thinking about disposability in relation to the community adds another facet to the question, that of its relation to individual members. A situation similar to that of overpopulated shelters is found within another of the "helping professions" (as far as I know that term ordinarily is applied only to people-helping professions, but why not to animal-helping as well?). I refer to nonprofit and public mental health clinics. Inevitably, more people need help than there are resources to provide it, and their needs are serious, ranging from family violence and suicide to disabling personality problems and sexual abuse of children. Creative, dedicated staffs have to innovate as their days fill: they schedule less frequent appointments with some clients and more group treatment, short-term interventions and support groups, work longer hours and seek out other resources. But time and schedules are finite and, in spite of all, they eventually fill and waiting lists grow—lists of people also with serious needs. What can "helpers" do?

One thing they cannot do is to jettison existing clients in order to empty the waiting list and keep the flow rolling. Section II.F. of the social worker's Code of Ethics says this: "The social worker's primary responsibility is to clients." Other sections speak of her responsibilities to the profession, colleagues, employers, and society—all of them important—but primacy remains with her existing clients, not the world of possible clients. The last would ask too much and interfere with the primary responsibility.

The ethical codes of seven other helping professions that I have reviewed (including psychiatrists, psychologists, and school counselors) place the same priority on their clients. This emphasis assuredly does not suggest indifference by these groups toward society or the community. I know from experience the strength of social work's social commitments. Rather, it says that the bonds of obligation that arise once the professional accepts another as her client become primary in relation to other responsibilities and other potential clients.

So disposability, or disposition in the larger sense, disturbs us when people enter relations implying commitment and we do not see it, or not enough. Commodity culture does not welcome commitments to anything before itself. This helps to explain, I suspect, how we can have the highest rates of charitable giving and volunteerism in the world combined with equally impressive levels of social dysfunction and pathology. These helping activities and sentiments know their place, which is somewhere down the scale from the truly important business of maximizing production and consumption.

When guardians troop into shelters to relinquish their companions because they have become inconveniences, we are not surprised. They simply act as the culture directs. Disposability is central within the reigning mythology—so much so that those who receive, adopt out, and otherwise dispose of animals need to be aware of their own part in sustaining the mythology. If disposability thrives under conditions of too little commitment, or the wrong kind, should not animal welfare examine its own commitments? For example, the discussion above about helping professions illustrates one resolution of the dilemma of caring for individuals while being dedicated to the community. In their case clients come first, but obligations to society and others remain strong nonetheless. In accepting animals into shelters where no space is left to keep them without killing an existing resident, whose interests are served? The individual animals involved? The present community of needy animals? The future such community? The human community? Whose?

One answer is that this practice attempts to care for both individual and community animals in that each one gets a chance, however brief, before new members of the community move in for their chance. And at the same time, suffering is relieved and prevented.

This response contains enough validity to have helped sustain the practice for quite a long time. But what does it say about the nature of the commitment to the killed animal who was healthy, not suffering, still adoptable but occupying a space wanted by another? If the dead had a voice he might wonder if he had not just suffered from disposability, part two. And when the relinquisher bothers to think about it, what might he or she conclude about the shelter's valuing of animals' lives? Are there not inconsistencies here with unintended consequences for long-term animal welfare? If shelter killing (when it is not euthanasia) enacts its own variety of animal disposability, thus facilitating cultural disposability, the time is now to reconsider institutional animal welfare's role in genuine animal welfare.

REFERENCES

Anchel, Marjorie (ed.). *Overpopulation of Cats and Dogs: Causes, Effects, and Prevention.* New York: Fordham University Press, 1990.

Anderson, Elizabeth. *Value in Ethics and Economics.* Cambridge: Harvard University Press, 1993.

Cross, Gary. *Time and Money: The Making of Consumer Culture.* New York: Routledge, 1993.

Hanke, Lewis. *Aristotle and the American Indians: A*

Study in Race Prejudice. Bloomington: Indiana University Press, 1959.

Kay, Michele. "Map Maker Folds." *Austin American-Statesman.* April 21, 1996, pp. B-1 & 6.

Lears, Jackson. *Fables of Abundance: A Cultural History of Advertising in America.* New York: Basic Books, 1994.

Muir, John. *The Yosemite.* San Francisco: Sierra Club Books, 1914.

Nash, Roderick. *Wilderness and the American Mind.* New Haven: Yale University Press, 1982, Third Edition.

Newmhan, Blaine. "A Living Museum." *Pacific Magazine,* January 28, 1996, pp. 8-15.

Porter, Eliot. *The Place No One Knew: Glen Canyon on the Colorado River.* Salt Lake City: Peregrine Smith Books, 1988.

Rivera, Luis. *A Violent Evangelism: The Political and Religious Conquest of the Americas.* Louisville: Westminster/John Knox Press, 1992. Citation from: Beatriz Pastor. *Discurso Narrativo de la Conquista de America.* La Habana: Casa de las Americas, 1984.

Rodman, John. "The Liberation of Nature?" *Inquiry* 20 (Spring 1977), pp. 89-90.

Schor, Juliet B. *The Overworked American.* New York: Basic Books, 1991.

Stannard, David. *American Holocaust.* New York: Oxford University Press, 1992.

4

VIEWS OF THE GOOD

In the discussion about disposing of the waste and cast-offs of everyday living, I mentioned those people for whom even that becomes a matter of concern because of their commitment to Earth and the community of life. Our concerns in disposing of the animals naturally go much deeper, but the example offers a good reminder of the importance of ultimate commitments as pole stars when we make choices and especially as we navigate difficult terrain. If animal shelters saw themselves primarily in the role of processing as many surplus animals as called upon (returning the lost, adopting out the unreclaimed or abandoned, euthanizing the unhealthy and unadoptable, humanely killing the remainder) in a kind of mechanical, socially-determined way, we would assume a primary commitment to efficiency and the status quo, regardless of the fine words surrounding the work. Fortunately, that is not the predominant attitude, although a suspicion of complacency is hard to avoid.

Before concluding, I want to think out loud for a few pages about ultimate commitments and their relation to our proximate commitments to companion animals. Inevitably this will be somewhat more personal than the rest, but I only wish to offer a view, not a model.

The disadvantage for a newcomer lies in his lack of history and experience within the field, but on the other hand he escapes some of the perils of habituation and brings fresh eyes to the scene. When I arrived at my new post working for animals I was not equipped with defenses specific to what would soon face me. So I was prepared by innocence, one could say, to respond with raw grief to what we were doing— much, I am sure, as most do when they come newly to the field. But it was not for me an unfamiliar feeling.

During most of the 1980s I had been director of a family counseling center, much of whose work was with clients of child welfare agencies: children abused, neglected, molested, or abandoned and who had seen and experienced what no one should. The Center had bought an old Victorian home and converted it to our main facility, with my office the former master bedroom at the head of the stairs and therapists' offices down the hall.

Friday afternoons were for group treatment of children, mostly girls, who had been sexually abused and who ranged from preschool age to adolescence. Several of the younger ones from various groups developed a ritual of dropping in as I worked at my desk. I knew generically what these children had experienced and with some I knew precisely. As they would end their visit to go to group I was usually left with a sadness leavened with admiration for the resiliency of these cheated creatures. The eyes of such children, like those of many animals arriving at our shelters, speak with a powerful silence: puzzlement, protest, inquisition, yearning. Voice of the vulnerable, I suppose we could call it. Seeing those familiar eyes was the first experience that told me the worlds of animal and child welfare might not be as different as expected.

Another came in similarities between respective "shelters." Fifteen years ago the city where my Center was based still held what were essentially old-fashioned orphanages. Begun around the turn of the century with the best of intentions, and for true orphans undoubtedly a blessing, they had evolved to taking in many children who were not orphaned but merely the unfortunate progeny of inept and irresponsible parents. Supposedly short-term, a respite while parents straightened out their difficulties, many of the kids lingered on in limbo, deteriorating steadily. Although these kinds of establishments hardly exist anymore, similar stories are not uncommon about children lost in a maze of foster homes. An over-enthusiastic desire to rescue these victims of parental failure had the unintended effect of further victimizing them and, as it very often happened, facilitating the parents' ongoing calamitous life courses. I once witnessed a most beautiful and beguiling five-year-old girl in one of these homes sink into clinical despair virtually before my eyes. I will not forget her, nor the parents I unsuccessfully attempted to reengage with her care. What kind of help was this?

And staffs have much in common. On average child welfare workers have more formal education than animal welfare workers, but on entry into their respective fields both groups tend to be young and idealistic, passionate about the well-being of their charges. They each face the occupational hazard of focusing so intently on protecting and advocating for their clients that they come to demonize and loathe those who have failed in their responsibilities. Hard to blame them, since many are truly loathsome. Nonetheless, those would-be parents and animal companions are not prone to accurate self-awareness and most will, one way or another, continue having children and/or animals. A long-term view to the welfare not just of the children and animals before our eyes but to future children and animals says these workers must contain their immediate feelings and think of the "adults" also as within their responsibility. They cannot reliably help the dependents without this longer view. Both sets of workers know this but have to struggle to remember it.

It is well recognized now that the dynamics and many of the individuals involved in child and animal abuse are pretty much the same; the discussion above only further illustrates commonalties. And as indicated earlier these and other forms of domination of the weak by the strong almost certainly emerge from a common foundation that raises the probabilities for such miscreant behavior. I am concerned to reduce these probabilities, to challenge their base in disposable culture, and to find alternatives to the tragic choice of killing healthy animals. To do this effectively those of us involved in victims' welfare will benefit from revisiting our ultimate commitments. For me that has occurred progressively over a number of years as I almost involuntarily, as it were, found myself moving toward an ethic that is more and more inclusive and that strives to offer active respect to whatever meets me along the way.

Long ago, to speak of ethics implied also a view of, or a search for, the Good: Good in the highest sense, as evidenced in practices, relationships, in lives as a whole. Effective teaching, learning, or doing of ethics, in fact, presupposed love of the Good. We have fallen a long way from such a strong and comprehensive sense of ethics as interwoven through the fabric of everyday life. But versions of that perspective remain, and I consider them helpful as we struggle toward revisioning our ways of best helping victims of disposability and dominance.

I think of Hans Jonas' ethic of responsibility, Paul Taylor's respect for biocentric equality, of recent work by feminist philosophers on ethics of care, and lastly of Martin Buber's emphasis on engagement and affirmation. These approaches have in common an insistence on the necessity for a sort of radical empathy ("to take an animal's standpoint," says Taylor) combined with an equally radical responsiveness—the determination to act consistent with that informed awareness of the other's being and needs.

Another tradition I draw on comes from what is called "virtue ethics." This concerns itself with the question of personal character, with those traits that conduce to doing right and achieving the Good. The "four cardinal virtues," for example, refer to prudence (the ability to see reality clearly and choose accordingly), temperance (the composing of oneself so as to act out of unity, humility, serenity), justice (to give to each his rightful due), and fortitude (patient endurance undeterred by compromise on what is vital). Although the virtues always imply certain ways of acting, they equally refer to being, to identity, to what Virginia Held called "the art of living a life." When one cares about virtue he cares about much more than simply discerning and following the rules.

These and other compatible approaches to ethics and animals (and we cannot forget Singer and Regan) are merely words: constructs and philosophies. Rarely are they transformative in themselves. More often than not they appear to be reports from the field, so to speak. The words describe experiences with children, animals, or other objects of care and try to generalize, explain, and defend the valid and compelling nature of those experiences. They are invaluable, but worthless without empathy and responsiveness. Without delivering ourselves back into renewed intimacy with the kinds of experiences that formed our care early on and with the ultimate commitments that germinated and grew from them, the words lose their cogency.

I left mental health and human services because I was losing the passion of those sensibilities, as many have who see problems worsened after two decades' effort. I think what was valuable for me in entering animal welfare was that prior sensitization to victims' plights and, as I said, no earlier need for desensitization to the new for me conditions at the animal shelter. I am urging here, finally, that animal welfare reopen to its fundamental sentiments and ultimate commitments, and to see where that might lead. Our "views of the Good" will be various in their particulars, but I cannot imagine them other than rigorous, responsible, and virtuous in the senses described. If they cannot meet that high standard, perhaps we are not involved in the mission we think we are.

REFERENCES

Buber, Martin. *Between Man and Man.* New York: Collier Books, 1965.

Held, Virginia (ed.). *Justice and Care: Essential Readings in Feminist Ethics.* Boulder: Westview Press, 1995.

Jonas, Hans. *The Imperative of Responsibility.* Chicago: University of Chicago Press, 1984.

Meilaender, Gilbert. *The Theory and Practice of Virtue.* Notre Dame: University of Notre Dame Press, 1984.

Pieper, Joseph. *The Four Cardinal Virtues.* Notre Dame: University of Notre Dame Press, 1983.

Taylor, Paul. *Respect for Nature: A Theory of Environmental Ethics.* Princeton: Princeton University Press, 1986.

5

FINAL THOUGHTS

Why animal shelters should not/cannot change significantly their existing practices:

- " They face a very complex and entrenched problem;
- " They are already doing many important things to solve the problem;
- " Their resources are limited;
- " Far more animals exist than homes to take them, and they probably always will;
- " Not to take in every animal brought to the shelter is to condemn the untaken to unspeakable fates of tremendous suffering, and whether adopted or killed these animals are spared such fates;
- " Many fine people work very hard at shelters and feel deeply about what they do and deserve support rather than criticism;
- " Criticism of shelter practice in fact risks increasing the problems;
- " Alternatives that have been offered are unacceptably risky.

I think that includes most aspects of the standard defense. Much of it is true and much highly speculative. As operational philosophy and self-representation, however, it gambles with insularity and self-fulfillment of dismal prophecies. If you believe, for example, that excess animals and killing them represent an unsolvable problem joined with an irrefutable solution, what hope can you offer? Criticism, even painful, far-reaching criticism, does not equal disrespect, but can provide the healthful tonic from which creative self-criticism can lead to fruitful change. But I will be honest: I have grown impatient with the sensitivities, self-righteousness, and ad hominem responses of many of those who most dogmatically propound the standard defense. Such reactions are unjust and unworthy of the mission and tasks before us. Alternatively, I earnestly hope to work with the willing toward saving lives and confronting the society that jeopardizes them.

Unintended Consequences

In the earlier discussion the problem of unintended consequences was addressed. I want to look at those consequences again, for the effort to do better for the animals depends first on facing the unintended downside of current practices. Only then are we in a position to seriously grapple with revising and revisioning. If this analysis is accurate, animal welfare operates not just in error, but counterproductively so.

Let me begin with an anecdote. One day last year I sat having my hair cut and listening as my barber chatted; he covers a lot of territory besides my head. In time he told me of his recent hunting trip. I responded in some fashion indicating that surely there were better things for him to do than unnecessarily end the lives of innocent wild animals. His immediate, vigorous, and I think heartfelt response was to remind me of what my shelter was doing to dogs and cats, and who was I to talk under those circumstances?

I could, of course, have tried to show the difference in the two situations and he could have talked about being a natural predator in tune with nature and no threat to the abundant species he preyed upon, and I could have mentioned overpopulation and suffering, etc. But we both would have missed the question of intrinsic value of animal lives, and in any event, my credibility as an advocate for animal welfare had been compromised.

The community of animal sheltering organizations occupies the paramount position, at least potentially, of being advocate and change agent for companion animals. But how persuasive can that community be so long as it speaks intrinsic value while concurrently sponsoring noneuthanasial killing of those same animals? Can we believe that this contradiction does not register on the public and most seriously dilute the life-affirming message that we intend? And if the message spoken by the animals' "best friends" is sufficiently diluted, do they end up prolonging the problem?

In discussing physician-assisted euthanasia of humans, some raise a related issue. They ask if allowing this professional, in whom we necessarily invest so much trust for care and cure, to participate in terminating a patient's life will not have the effect of insidiously damaging doctor-patient relationships. Can I the patient, in other words, maintain my confidence in one who may be mixing his determination to help me heal with thoughts of helping me painlessly exit? I don't see that this must be the case. It becomes problematic only when one questions the motivations and judgment of family and physician, which is to say when they may not truly be contemplating euthanasia but rather a killing to serve other interests. A physician's gift of euthanasia will not trouble us but his/her commitment to anything other than maximum care certainly will raise anxieties and doubts. In like manner, the public is sure to recognize at some level that not all the animal killing serves animal interests as much as it does others'.

But this does not say all that needs saying. Those concerns about physicians crossing the line from saving to terminating lives approach what might be the central reality underlying discussions such as these. When the subject is humans and their own euthanasia, there hovers around it a sense of human life as sacred and of how best to express respect for that life. I want to take it farther. That anything exists at all seems to me the most inexplicable and value-laden thing. The bare fact of life—to have journeyed from the fifteen-billion-year-old primordial irruption to a Yosemite Valley and a plethora of species—can capture our awe. Our reverence should start with life rather than niggling down to only human life. Not just any life is preferable to no life, obviously, but life itself still remains the grand reality, not to be deliberately obliterated until so little valuable endures that respect calls for attending to its gentle passage into death. If those who include nonhuman animal life within this expanded purview of respect wish to be persuasive with that conviction, they have great reason to reevaluate their bearings, methods, and ultimate aspirations within the clear light of that conviction.

The first unintended consequence of shelter killing, then, is diminished credibility and influence due to the incongruence between words and actions. Linked with this is the problem of mixed messages wherein the listener selects for compatibility with his own dispositions. The second unintended consequence, closely allied with the first and connected specifically with the always open receiving door, pertains to the likelihood that when they offer the convenience of animal welfare "rescuing" of guardian-relinquished animals, welfarists inadvertently reinforce disposability. There are at least three self-defeating parts to the dynamics of this interchange.

The first is the question of professional ethics: What are the priority obligations of a helping professional toward existing and potential clients? As mentioned, helpers of humans have uniformly answered the question in favor of existing clients while animal welfare has taken the more expansive position of "serving" all comers even when that means killing some for space. I submit that this looks like what it is—a betrayal of the animals already taken into care. If someone responds that animals are more vulnerable than humans, have fewer resources and face greater dangers, I recommend he spend a few hours in the waiting room of a public clinic and read the initial assessments and diagnoses on the waiting list. It seems the sad case that our society spews out more casualties, human and nonhuman, than there ever will be resources to care for properly so long as society remains unchanged. Is it not a better response to extend our critique of animal devaluation toward its roots, to reconsider what it means to take responsibility for a life, and simultaneously to be sure that we do not in any way unconsciously participate in devaluation?

The second part is well known by effective parents and anyone psychologically healthy who has ever been close to an alcoholic: Rescuing people from the consequences of their irresponsible behavior offers an excellent means to see more of that behavior. People take on animals—casually, impulsively, carelessly, uncommitedly—then want relief from the burden, at least for the present. And with that attitude they obviously should not have an animal (although they almost certainly will again, sooner or later). But what do they learn when they desert their companion at the shelter on their way to the mall, or out of town, or to the new apartment? Something about disposability, I think, and not what we wish. If shelters want to alter this behavior they must do more than exhort about guardian responsibility. They must expect it and help provide the means to bring it about.

Lastly, most relinquishing guardians feel guilty, as they should. There is an optimal, change-motivating level of guilt that anyone who has done wrong should experience, and I wish that level for all these people. But I fear that when the caretakers at the humane society assume guardians' responsibility, that guilt becomes easier to shed. Denial and other preferred defense mechanisms are always available, and when the people acknowledged as having the best interests of animals at heart assume one's burden, can the relinquisher more comfortably feel his duty fulfilled?

The third unintended consequence relates to motivational pressure to change, to be innovative in an active search for promising alternatives. Today, killing the excess preserves the balance between live animals and numbers of available homes and shelter spaces. The number killed rises and falls depending on demand, and except for the ravaged emotions of shelter workers, it seems an efficient, efficacious machine, something like a recycling center, as a board member once put it. But does it work too well? If the streets are cleansed of straying animals and mangled bodies (as they should be), and guardians have nonstigmatized means of abandoning their animals for others to dispose of, where is the inherent pressure to change? Ironically, "relieving suffering" of today's excess animals may well result in the prolongation of killing as society finds expedient disposition of animals preferable to the bother of changing itself. Shelter workers feel the strain of this solution most strongly, but they are powerless and convinced of unending necessity. This has about it that odd aspect within contemporary "power" medicine which has devoted itself to increasingly exotic, intrusive, and expensive diagnostics and treatments while neglecting prevention. Killing healthy animals is a treatment that does not cure.

One response to this analysis will point to the probability that all kinds of services, from AFDC to health insurance to psychotherapy, have unintended consequences. Witness the connection between insurance and mushroomed health care costs or the tendency of some to use aid or therapy as a means of avoiding or externalizing responsibility. These endeavors no doubt have those effects, but usually tangentially and always fought. The difference within animal welfare is that contradictions go to the heart of the enterprise and help to defeat its larger purposes and subvert its deepest values.

With these thoughts in mind I offer the following suggestions. The changes fall within the general categories of program, strategy, and identity.

Program

The three fundamental shelter themes—sterilization, adoption, and increased guardian responsibility—cover the terrain well, insofar as they are ambitiously conceived and promoted. But any organization that sees the present situation as unacceptable and urgent in its claim on our efforts will continuously examine itself critically, with eyes focused on excellence. Many organizations in other fields are responsible to accrediting bodies that regularly force this sort of self-examination and bring outside eyes to the process. The community of shelters could benefit from such oversight. In lieu of that they must demand of themselves that 1) the message and the means for comprehensive spay/neutering are as thoroughly broadcast as their resources allow and that no animal leaves them unaltered, and 2) that education toward morally mature responsibility in the relationship of guardian to animal is promoted similarly, partly through the assistance of volunteer animal advocates. These things are noncontroversial and require only that complacency be driven out and urgency planted in its stead.

The third area, shelter adoption, perhaps even more than the others, demands extra scrutiny. Is it predestined that the shelter share of animal placements remain so low? Why do shelters with major decreases in incoming animals so often remain stagnant in their adoption levels? Whatever our own feelings about them, shelters generally are not cheerful places. We should strive, insofar as possible, to make them so, but just as important to find outside venues and unconventional means for announcing availability and taking the animals to potential adopters. Imagine what an increase in "market share" of only a few percentage points would mean to shelter adoption levels, not to mention to the adoptees.

Adoption standards need clarification, and the handling of the adoption interchange between shelter worker and public must be vastly improved. The question of standards invokes great passion, as it should, for we do not achieve the consistency I recommend if care and education are not strongly involved in making a match. The problem arises with the "marginals"—adopters who seem to offer less than the best but who, in words from child welfare, may be "good enough" companions under the extant circumstances of over-population. As mentioned earlier, when people like this leave empty-handed and angry, shelters lose the possibility of an ongoing educative relationship. And the adopter will almost certainly find another animal elsewhere who may remain fertile, unlike one from the shelter. Follow-up on placements with these people by volunteers provides an excellent use of their energies.

Plainly stated, shelters that accept animals when full and kill for space, and who turn away such people, should consider how often they precipitate not just an immediate death but others unknown in the form of offspring from the animal acquired away from the shelter.

Finally, as an animal organization executive director, my major source of grief, aside from dead or abused animals, arose from the encounter between would-be adopters and shelter adoption counselors. The interchange produces immense heat, some of it unavoidable due to the clash in perceptions regarding the nature of what is going on, purchase vs. adoption (within a culture that tends to regard most any-thing as consumable). Not uncommonly the temperature rises to boil and near violence, and complaints to adminis-trators come frequently. Not every criticism has to be con-strued as gospel to recognize that most provide some piece of information from which staffs can learn. Shelter culture is insular, though, born mostly I suppose from the concur-rence of rescuing, loving, and often killing animals, and the predisposition is to discount complaints, blaming the com-plainer. Selection, training, assignment, and supervision of staff, who are mostly young, underpaid, and overworked, are far short of what is needed, else the problems would be less persistent and frequent. We should not accept this level of malfunction, or treat it as somehow inherent and un-changeable. That contact between "us" and "them" may be the most telling of all in our success as organizations (think of p.r., fundraising, good will, and so on) and most impor-tantly, as organizations with lives dependent on their effec-tiveness.

Strategy

I call this area strategy but it may be more accurate to think of as bridging the space between program and strat-egy. I am inclined to think that no matter how much pro-grammatic excellence we accomplish, it will not be enough nor as prompt and lasting as desired without strategic risk-taking of the sort I now want to discuss. These concern han-dling guardian-releases, the practice of killing, and chal-lenging both broad cultural values and specific, discernible actors within it who aggravate the problems.

Not all animals who approach the shelter are alike. They come with different burdens and liabilities, and those who are stray and those guardian-accompanied present animal welfare with different challenges and possibilities. Today's shelter practice gives the appearance of one designed for stray animals but into which guardian- releases have come to be inserted alongside. Strays are those most vulnerable (and most often referenced in the standard defense) to suf-fering and violent death. Unless the shelter can place them in good homes, they have no place to be beyond foster homes and the shelter. They are, or become, prime candidates for euthanasia, for their suffering often is far from hypothetical.

Guardian-accompanied animals, however, are not yet homeless, and though almost certainly not well nurtured are rarely faced with "fates worse than death." I recommend that no guardian-releases be accepted at shelters unless they present a case of clear-and-present danger of abuse or abandonment. Rather, they should be counseled about alternatives: management of allergies or behavior problems; redirection to "pet friendly" landlords; taking responsibility for arranging their own adoption under advice of shelter staff; use of computer and old-fashioned bulletin boards and other media for announcing the animal's availability to a worthy new companion; going on the waiting list if all else fails until space opens at the shelter or a foster home. Shelter consistency around the disposability issue demands that releases become less convenient. If we really believe in guardian responsibility, this is a place to begin teaching it, even if it means only that they take responsibility for finding a new companion more responsible than themselves.

I know the objection. These animals will be abandoned, abused, killed; they will suffer grievously. But how do we know that, how do we accurately predict, for how many will that happen? The fact is, I do not know and I know of no one who does, what the odds are for animals in this situation who would be handled as I recommend. But we certainly do know the fates of many who are taken in and disposed of under the current regime. Having that knowledge, and believing as we say we do about the value of all life, we are obliged to face this uncertainty openly and to become more discriminating. As it is, shelters trade off a vast number of certain deaths to ward off an indeterminate amount of speculative suffering. Where did we learn that all guardians relinquishing were not simply irresponsible (probably) but evil, unimaginative, and utterly uncooperative as well? To whatever extent they may act in some of those ways, what part do current receiving practices encourage or enable it?

In the process of promoting shelter consistency about guardian responsibility and animal disposability, this policy of reduced receptivity in receiving would strengthen our messages about those issues. Walk must match talk, as they say, if the words would be honored. At the same time, with receiving numbers down, there would be more time for training and placing the known sufferers, the more thoroughly victimized strays.

Despite the uncertainties, in all likelihood some animals who might have been painlessly killed will end up painfully abused and dead anyway. But the risk must be faced; current practice has not worked, and this can be one lane of the road out of our dilemmas and animals' tragedies. Should it turn out the wrong one, we would know it and we would learn and we would try again. Not just any life is better than death, but if I am in the place of the animal I assuredly hope death becomes a last resort only after others have clearly failed. I would rather take a chance on suffering than experience unnecessary or pointless death.

That brings us to euthanasia and humane killing. As has been said here many times, true euthanasia provides one means by which one's devotion to the welfare of another finds fulfillment, however sadly. Beyond that, killing enters troubled waters. Presumably the goal of relieving suffering has surpassed that of saving life since animal welfare's beginnings. At times that has probably been for excellent reasons associated with the circumstances of those beginnings. Our question now must be whether it is either right or effective to continue killing under *today's* circumstances. For all of the reasons described above and in light of the continued high mortality rates at most shelters, I believe noneuthanasial killing has become counterproductive. I suggest that if our first commitment is to animal welfare, all such killing should cease. To aim to relieve suffering in the absence of an equally intense commitment to save lives opens the way for endless rationalization and apparently endless killing.

What will happen to all those animals? If we are doing our jobs programmatically, if we are educating and advocating vigorously, if we change the receiving sign to "advising and assisting," the better question becomes, What will happen to *the numbers* of all those animals? They will fall. We do not know how far, but we need to find out. Mother necessity must begin to invent. We will find anew what we are made of; we will do better than we do now. If society finds it more convenient to continue killing, then society will have to take responsibility for doing the killing itself. Animal welfare shelters would euthanize in only the true sense, and nothing lethal beyond that.

I am aware of the criticisms of "no-kills": warehousing, skimming the adoptable cream, depending on others to do the dirty work, low adoption standards, manipulation of facts and numbers. Many critics seem to believe that no-kills are universally and perhaps inherently subject to these failures. I do not know the degree of truth in the allegations (who does?), but where accurate they definitely challenge those organizations to change. But the criticisms are not germane here. To begin with, I am only urging "no-noneuthanasial-killing." And if programmatic excellence accompanies the change, as intended, the alleged probabilities of failure would not find fertile ground in which to root.

Finally, knowing the opposition this suggestion will arouse, I ask why so many would remain so determined that animal welfare be the killing site? Society, after all, if it wishes, can work its own will in its own facilities. The answer to the question, I suppose, will be that only shelter welfarists would reliably bring skill and compassion to the task. But how plausible is that today, and are there territorial issues muddying these waters? Indeed, organizations in general are notoriously hesitant to relinquish control in an area which has been theirs.

The last aspect of the dimension I am calling strategy concerns animal welfare's posture toward those who tend to oppose or sabotage positive efforts for animal welfare. What are their effects on advancing or impeding respectful relations with animals? These include pet stores that continue selling companion animals, deliberate and accidental breeders, certain pet supply marketing tactics, and those veterinarians who fail to use their knowledge and influence to educate about overpopulation and general animal well-being. If we decide that our primary responsibility is to our animal "clients" and that others are acting detrimentally to them, how can we excuse failing to protest and advocate in a strong, unambiguous, and unrelenting fashion?

This raises a question that will help move us into the final issue of animal welfare identity. As was discussed earlier, we can hardly fail to recognize that we operate within a culture that anchors commodity values and relationships firmly at its center. This could not succeed without its simultaneously marginalizing contrary values such as reverence and respect for multiple goods and expressions of life. Those committed to values and experiences of the latter sort—such as toward nature, spirit, communities of humans and animals—face real dilemmas in their participation within and attitudes toward opposing cultural forces. Those holding such values are, in a sense, extremist. To affirm, for example, that the life of a dog must elicit the same moral consideration as a human life, and to say it within a cultural context that in practice lacks conviction about even human moral worth—such affirmation speaks a delegitimized voice. If we would avoid cooptation by commodification, we must face the implications of our "extremist" commitments.

The strategic implication of these suggestions and also of our commitments is this: We take a stronger, more adamant stand; we do not simply exhort about guardians' responsibility, but cease relieving them of it; we act consistently as believers in the intrinsic value of lives; we refuse to kill the still-healthy victims; we pointedly confront forces of victimization. Animal welfare must decide who it is and what it means to accomplish. The dichotomy between notions of suffering relief and life saving reaches beyond conceptions of what's possible and on into the character of animal welfare's deepest convictions.

Identity

A Hasidic story from Martin Buber tells of Rabbi Zusya speaking shortly before his death: "In the world to come I shall not be asked: 'Why were you not Moses?' I shall be asked: 'Why were you not Zusya?'"

A few weeks ago my local paper reported on a "bird drop" occurring as part of festivities in a Texas panhandle town. Guineas, flightless barnyard birds, are dropped from an airplane, one with a $100 bill strapped to his leg. Instinctively they glide downward and are then pursued by celebrants after the money. The local humane society director claimed to have looked into the practice "and none of the birds seemed to be affected by it. So we don't have a problem with what they're doing."

Who *is* animal welfare? I suppose every social change movement has participants ranging from close to status quo, to moderates, and on to radicals. And tensions rise among them. Probably inevitable, this situation may even be fruitful as it can force each camp to periodically reexamine itself. The circumstances within animal welfare, however, seem to me drastically more imperative, meriting a "radical" approach for at least two reasons. First, only there does one see adherents killing the movement's failures. And second, it seems uniquely positioned for success. Both these considerations ought to raise motivation and mobilize believers finally to accomplish their ancient goals. But an identity oriented around suffering relief will be something other than one oriented around life preservation. The latter demands much more.

One way of looking at the approach and recommendations of this essay will see it as a striving after consistency— a consistency that begins with our core verbal commitments and follows them to what seems their natural conclusion. The conviction of life's (and lives') intrinsic value is not simply an idle predilection, a matter of taste or opinion. It seems impossible to me that one could truly come to that conviction and remain unchanged otherwise. As said above, it is an inherently radical belief within the present context, and it places demands on the believer.

By way of comparison I think of a contemporary group much of whose philosophy and tactics I do not accept but who do exhibit consistency, at times to an extreme. These are the radical "pro-life" people who can often be found surrounding clinics that provide abortions. I need not admire these people overall to recognize that based on their core conviction of the sacredness of life from conception, it naturally follows that most abortion is murder (or at least deeply wrong). I would prefer that they recognize what seems to me the inherent existential and moral ambiguity of gestational life but they do not, and they picket and confront instead, as their convictions require.

I speak of the "pro-life" movement despite my discomfort with it because it illustrates so well the expression of a firm consistency in following through on the intrinsic demand character of focal values. Earth First! and certain animal rights activists would do as well. It seems today that by definition animal welfare's identity lacks the "punch," the adamancy, of other change seekers. And this is odd. The good that is sought for animal companions and the ethics underlying that good are hardly so laden with inexorable ambiguities as abortion.

Animal welfare's true identity will be formed as it begins to take more seriously the implications of its expressed commitments. That will be difficult. Not only the content of the commitments but unrelenting pursuit of ethical goods in general are contrary to the spirit of our times. But lives, and relief of real suffering, depend upon it. It does not follow that identical responses will emerge from self-definition. We need diversity within our unity—though not just any forms will do. Like Rabbi Zusya, we must operate authentically in relation to the greater Good that we envision.

6

AFTERWORD

I began the preceding part of this book when the organization where I was executive director, the Progressive Animal Welfare Society, was starting its preparations to move to a "no kill" posture. We spent most of 1995 working on programs to accomplish the changes we knew would be necessary to reduce the numbers of homeless animals. On January 1, 1996 the change became official. Among the efforts we undertook were these:

1. Adoption outreach through veterinary clinics, pet supply stores, and television and radio spots;
2. Photo boards of available animals and adoption kiosks at a number of locations around the city;
3. Colored flyers with animal pictures posted weekly at almost 200 locations;
4. Summer Sundays saw foster care volunteers take animals to the park for adoptions and to offer animal behavior advice;
5. Cable television daily carried a half hour program featuring available animals;
6. A PAWS Home Page through the internet provided pictures and information about animals in need of homes;
7. Improvements in managing the lost-and-found system were implemented;
8. Expanded foster care;
9. Developing a system for handling guardian-re-

lease requests where efforts to solve the problems come first, placement on a waiting list if relinquishment is unavoidable could follow, and efforts are made to assist guardians in arranging their own adoptions;

10. Expansion of the spay/neuter clinic to provide low cost surgeries for the general public, including promotional efforts aimed at reaching pre-pubescent animals.

Perhaps as important as all of this was the change in the atmosphere. A new optimism and positive energy appeared as staff developed a sense of solving rather than simply managing companion animal problems.

Unfortunately for me, I had to leave PAWS in January 1996. Unexpected family contingencies arose that took me to Texas. But I continued working on the book and in the summer of '96 began collaborating with folks who had read the manuscript and thought it could help to encourage new thinking and urgency within animal welfare. These were Mitchell Fox from PAWS, Kim Sturla of the Fund for Animals, Ed Sayres of American Humane Association, and Diane Allevato of Marin Humane Society. In February 1997 they hosted a meeting in Denver of twenty representatives of national, regional, and local animal-related organizations to discuss issues facing animal welfare.

After two days of discussions the walls were covered with overlapping flip chart pages. The first quarter of the time was spent identifying the group's core convictions: those fundamental beliefs we hold about the nature of reality, specifically that aspect of it pertaining to our relations with the larger-than-human world. In summary, those convictions follow:

- There is a tapestry of all living things for which we have respect and reverence.
- All living things have intrinsic value, and interests separate from human perspective.
- Animals are sentient creatures.
- We live and act in a manner that does the least possible harm and the greatest possible good.
- We act in a truthful and honest way with ourselves

and others.

" We recognize that there are different strategies that conscientious and principled people may choose to approach our common goals, and we agree to treat these people respectfully.

For the remainder of the two days we talked about "critical issues" facing animal welfare:

1. Do animal shelters contribute to the notion that dogs and cats are disposable by taking in unwanted animals and "euthanizing" those for whom they cannot find homes?

2. How can humane organizations most effectively use their resources to address overpopulation and other companion animal problems; in particular, should they continue their level of involvement in animal sheltering and other animal control functions?

3. Are humane organizations inconsistent when they do not address issues affecting noncompanion animals, since other animals suffer abuse and exploitation as well?

4. Do humane organizations, from complacency, fear of offending donors, or for other reasons, fail to bring the creativity, passion, and energy to their efforts at helping animals that the problems and their expressed values would call for?

The discussions were good and often spirited. As I write this a few days afterward, however, it is still hard to say how much was accomplished. The readiness to consider bold new approaches continues to be constrained for some by the weight of tradition and fear of change and its possible consequences for needy animals. On the other hand, nearly everyone seemed to agree that self-evaluation and reexamination of organizational priorities and practices need to be undertaken and that efforts to encourage the field at large to begin doing so are worth attempting. And that is where things stand this late winter in early '97.

I close this part of the book with an invitation to readers. Obviously I intend this effort to be a part of (and perhaps something of a catalyst to) more extensive efforts to stir the waters of animal welfare. I believe that renewed commitment and more strenuous advocacy for our values and goals can, to a considerable extent, carry the day for companion animals.

Part of this involves keeping a conversation going among animal advocates. I welcome responses, pro or con, to what you have read here. I also want to hear from people who have knowledge of initiatives aimed at solving animal overpopulation that you know to be particularly effective. Whether dealing with spaying and neutering, adoptions, lost-and-found, education, legislation, advocacy, or responses to the problem of guardian-releases, let me hear about them. I plan a follow-up publication to this book in which I will incorporate these ideas and hope thereby to facilitate their distribution to people who might not otherwise hear about them. You can reach me through the publisher whose address is on the copyright page.

Finally, if you are still looking for an organizational vehicle for your desire to help out the animals, check the appendix. It is by no means a complete list, but it is a good sample and starting place. They can use your support.

PART TWO

RELATIONS WITH NONCOMPANION ANIMALS

7

THE SPORT OF HUNTING

Dried viscera. Liver, gall, kidneys. The inward parts of the beast who dreams of man and has so dreamt in running dreams a hundred thousand years and more. Dreams of that malignant lesser god come pale and naked and alien to slaughter all his clan and kin and rout them from their house. A god insatiable whom no ceding could appease nor any measure of blood.

The old man went on to say that the hunter was a different thing than men supposed. He said that men believe the blood of the slain to be of no consequence but that the wolf knows better.... Finally he said that if men drink the blood of God yet they do not understand the seriousness of what they do. He said that men wish to be serious but they do not understand how to be so. Between their acts and their ceremonies lies the world and in this world the storms blow and the trees twist in the wind and all the animals that God has made go to and fro yet this world men do not see. They see the acts of their own hands or they see that which they name and call out to one another but the world between is invisible to them.

Cormac McCarthy, *The Crossing*

The average columnist in a newspaper "Outdoors" section (Hunting and Fishing) lapses into foot-stamping, sputtering incredulity when the average animal rights advocate crosses his horizon. The advocate seems as incomprehensible to the columnist as would the appearance of Bigfoot singing opera. So when the Make-A-Wish Foundation decided in the spring of 1996 to satisfy a mortally ill adolescent's dream of hunting an Alaskan bear, and animal advocates protested, it brought a predictable howl from my local scribe. His vexation was headlined, "Spoilsports try to ruin a sick boy's dream wish."

Lost on the columnist was a contradiction. The Foundation agreed to honor the tragic prematurity of a boy's unavoidable death through the willed prematurity of a bear's arranged death. The preciousness of one life memorialized through the taking of another's.

A striking feature of modern morality arises when people who claim to believe in the importance of strong moral convictions find themselves challenged on strong moral grounds. They often regress into relativism. This is particularly common in responses to animal rights assertions. So the columnist depreciates objections to the bear's killing as simply "personal views on hunting," as if all views were only opinions, one as good as another. To his credit he did not add the usual accusation confusing advocacy with "trying to force their views upon others." And he did offer offhand a defense of his views: "Bear hunting is legal, and it's not immoral....There is substantial biological support for bear hunting....He [the boy] isn't going to do harm to another human being." The defense rests on legality, biology, and the unique moral status of humans.

Since legality and morality are built on different foundations, and what the law allows morality sometimes forbids, the columnist does well not to conflate them. He is right: one may legally kill a bear, even without provocation. The argument from biology presumably refers to the healthy numbers of the species population in Alaska (leave aside what historically hunters did to these bears south of there), meaning that "harvesting" a few will not threaten overall viability of the survivors. This also is true but ethically irrelevant in the situation at hand. On this ground, viable over-populated *Homo sapiens* could be thinned. The clincher here, as so often elsewhere, comes with the third item: the unique loftiness of human moral status and the dramatic plunge downward required to sound out the status of every other living being. Since human value has been elevated (by humans) so far above that of all our earthly co-existents, we receive considerations not granted the others.

This assumed hierarchy, though ancient and nearly universal, fails to disguise its oddity within the entwinements of this world—evolutionary, ecological, ethical, spiritual. Spawn of identical elements, equally reliant on the same nature's community of being, all embedded in a shared and mysterious reality: from where came the massive human moral priority relative to all the other creatures?

I want to examine this within the sport of hunting, for it seems so unnecessary and troubling to inflict this violence upon an already deeply violated nature. Further, having friends and family who hunt, I am perplexed by the casual acceptance of this enterprise that seems to me so unacceptable.

The Lives of Bears

I discover in my dictionary that "sport" has an interesting progression of meanings. It begins as a skilled athletic activity and ranges on through pleasant pastime, recreation, jest, mockery and derision, and then this: "something or someone treated lightly or tossed about like a plaything." What should one make of these meanings?

Sport hunting is often recommended as one form of skilled athleticism and among a few it surely is. But the gravity of sporting endeavors significantly declines after that. Sport becomes activities of little consequence, and the objects of sport are not taken seriously. Even skilled athleticism, as we often hear in reference to professional sports, "is only a game." We begin to see from this that sport represents mere diversion. But as embodied in hunting, inconsequential activity erupts as killing, certainly among the most serious choices a person can make. A fundamental incoherence appears, and one might conclude that hunting was mistakenly preserved historically as it degenerated into sport, for death is no proper diversion.

A hunter should know his victim, give him a face, discover a personality (animality). Who, then, are these bears, these expendable creatures our columnist and unfortunate boy have in mind to kill? Their evolution began thirty million years ago as meat-eating, tree-climbing mammals, probably not much bigger than a terrier. They emerged as biologically true bears from large dogs in North America. The genus *Ursus* arose two and a half million years ago in Europe and arrived in the Western Hemisphere via the Bering land bridge. *Ursus arctos*, the brown bear and object of our immediate interest, is more widely distributed around the world than any other bear. Early this century they were thought to consist of dozens of species but now are considered only one with perhaps a subspecies in the Kodiak Islands.

Any particular bear begins in a mating that occurs in spring or early summer. This may be virtually all the social contact the shy and solitary male will have all year. Through the wisdom of nature the embryo will not implant until fall, and then only if mother has had a healthy and nutritionally adequate summer to carry her through the rigors of pregnancy and birth. After no more than two months' gestation, a blind, nearly naked one-pounder (or two, three, sometimes four of them) leaves the comfort of womb for the den. He grows quickly and when weather permits in the spring mother and young venture forth. He has a better than 60% chance of reaching adulthood. With luck his earthly tenure may last thirty years, but few can count on it.

Anyone who has hiked in Alaska will confirm that bear country, which all of it is, feels different than lands without them. The virtues of alertness are newly appreciated. One author speaks of bears as "a unique combination of power and poetry" and suggests that our proper response lies in a balance of knowledge with awe.

Like ourselves they are subject to frailties of the body. Arthritis to tuberculosis, dental caries to hemorrhoids: the mighty, too, are bound to our common physicality. On the exterior, the "mitey" are no respecter of rank, as lice, ticks, and fleas find their anointed places while a variety of worms grovel beneath the skin. Life feasts on life. These creatures have no choices.

Bears see well (contrary to general belief), hear well, and

have the olfactory sensitivity of a dog, maybe better. Considering their evolutionary relatedness, that does not surprise. Their intelligence is said by some to rival that of many primates. With a curiosity that ranges beyond the simply instrumental and demonstrated capacities for rapid learning, these great creatures are far from brutish. They move massively over the land, but when caution is advisable they can magically hide themselves and have been known to take care to disguise their trail. Apparently, they also have an attachment to home as they have defeated efforts to transplant them by boat and air, determinedly finding their way back. Subsequent evictions are often manhandled fatally.

Many animals, bears among them, have developed ways of managing potentially violent situations with minimal or no injurious conflict. This is fascinating, particularly considering our frequent use of the epithet "animal" pejoratively and our own overuse and mismanagement of aggression. Those observers are right who say that one of the chief tasks facing society involves the socialization of male humans. Our younger ones especially are violent and getting more so, and perhaps can learn from the so-called brutes. Where codes of "honor" among some of us demand violence, these other animals retain their integrity more peaceably.

The costs of aggression, near and long term, usually exceed the benefits. Bears know this. When encounter occurs, as at a salmon-filled stream or on a trail, a hierarchical sorting takes effect: big guys over smaller, male over female (unless she has cubs). Ambiguity produces ritual, posturing, a bit of skirmish with ordinarily little damage. Each gets fed or goes on his way, self-esteem and body still intact. Try those approaches in certain urban streets or country bars and see what happens. The intelligence of nonviolence has yet to receive adequate appreciation within our species.

An alternative or sometimes corollary to these hierarchies is known as ignoring. Step aside, avoid eye contact, or turn away and the aggression index holds steady or diminishes and life goes on unscathed. My personal bear story involves a cub treed by my dog, who soon found herself desperate for my company as mother bear came forth in pursuit. As dog retreated behind me and bear stood before, I remained utterly still, every cell humming beatific peace and good will. Had she chosen, I was breakfast. Whether from simple kindness or recognition that I honored the hierarchy between us, she turned back and I retreated with only my nerves in tatters.

We should think about this contrast between bears' management of aggression and that of humans. Our heedlessness compared to their discretion needs explanation, particularly in light of that boy making-a-wish and his companion hunters making theirs. Sport killing.

A Defense of Hunting

Traditional Hebrew mythology, in fear and reverence, forbids speaking the name of God. Similarly, among Arctic peoples the grizzly could only be spoken of as "the Great One." Whether peacefully abiding as neighbors or at the time of the necessary hunt, reverential etiquette imposed expectations: to give what's due to the spirit and life of this beast, this numinous being.

Do bears have "lives"?

Life is the fundamental good, usually better than death and prerequisite for all other goods. As Thoreau put it so well: "Every creature is better alive than dead, men and moose and pine-trees, and he who understands it aright will rather preserve its life than destroy it." Bears have lives, not mere lumpish existences. They have a place, a role, a way.

Do bears have "goods"?

How could we doubt it? How could we doubt that in his way the bear rejoices in life as I in my way rejoice in mine? It is surely nonsense writ large to think him indifferent toward the unique goods of his life or that he has no direction, awareness, or way of flourishing, to think he merely endures life in resigned fulfillment of biological imperatives. Knowing these things and knowing our desire to hold on to our own lives, are there valid reasons for unnecessarily taking his?

Some think so. Richard Nelson, for example, is a hunter whose sensibilities toward nature I almost completely share, although for him they branch off to permit what for me they forbid. An anthropologist turned nature writer/philosopher,

Nelson was deeply influenced by time he spent with Eskimos and later with Koyukon Indians in Alaska. Their view, and now his, is of "a code of moral and ethical behavior that keeps a hunter in right relationship to the animals. They [traditional Koyukon] teach that all of nature is spiritual and aware, that it must be treated with respect, and that humans should approach the living world with restraint and humility." As I read his writing I hear his determination to live this code.

Strictly speaking I am not sure it is altogether accurate to include Nelson among sport hunters. His thoughtfulness and humility along with de-emphasized self-gratifications from the hunt are inconsistent with the approach represented by the newspaper columnist and those to whom he speaks. Nonetheless, by neither culture nor necessity is he a subsistence hunter. The native peoples from whom he learned still lived close to their subsistence origins, and the hunt and ways of life in which it participated resonated with that history. Why does this sensitized Westerner choose to hunt?

In "The Gifts of Deer" I find two explanations. He says that as a younger man he thought hunting immoral; he loved animals with his eyes only. But later, expressing this love through student scientific study, he felt barriers of detachment and abstraction arise. Then he gravitated to anthropology, experienced native ways of life and teachings, and found the intimate connectedness with nature that he sought. For those people he so much admired, hunting was sustenance for body and soul. He took up a gun alongside them.

He describes two moving encounters with deer in the essay (which occurs at some remove in time and space from the Koyokon; he lives in Alaska's Southeast, the panhandle lying between Canada and the Pacific). In one he kills a buck, and in the other he chooses only to get close, so close that in her befuddlement from the rut and attentions of a nearby buck, a doe comes so near he touches her on the head before she flees in horror at her momentary lack of caution. He compares the experiences and allows that they might seem contradictory, "but they are in fact identical. Both are founded in the same principles, the same relationship, the same reciprocity." Apparently, a large part of this reciprocity consists in the deer's "giving" himself to the hunter rather than being taken; he repeats this notion several times in the essay. His part in the exchange would be respect, humility, and gratitude.

Attractive as Nelson's sensitivities to nature are, the idea of these two encounters as identically reciprocal and of the deer *giving* his life to the hunter perplexes me. In what meaningful sense can we think peaceful engagement identical with violent extirpation of a life? In both settings he was deeply focused and alert, appreciative (in different ways, maybe for different reasons) of the proximity and power of the deer. But the intrinsically valued relation of quiet beholding and letting be seems far more respectful than the other relation, a relation of violent intrusion and use—stalk, kill, butcher, eat—even if grateful use. The only way these relations can be considered identical, as far as I can tell, is by deleting the sting of death, by leveling out beholding and killing. Suppose the deadly encounter had been reversed and the buck had turned, charged, and slain the hunter. Would Ms. Nelson have considered the meetings as "the same relationship?" (Actually, the peaceful encounter would not have occurred since the violent one came first, which itself is interesting to think about: violence forecloses more than we know.)

In what sense did the deer "give" his life to the hunter? Should we think of this as we do of a soldier "giving" his life for his country? No, for soldiers mostly only "risk" their lives which are then sometimes "taken," and they surely do not wish to give anything to the adversary. Nelson speaks of receiving nurturance (the second reason for hunting) and that's certainly a kind of gift—but hard to imagine freely given. Just prior to the statement about reciprocity he says this: "Two deer came and gave the choices to me. One deer I took and we will now share a single body. The other deer I touched and we will now share that moment." Choice belonged to Nelson, but was it of receiving or taking? And do we imagine the deer indifferent to his decisions?

No one credibly argues anymore for meat's necessity to a healthy diet. Meat is a choice, not necessity nor even need.

As such, one who makes that choice assumes a moral burden—to deprive a fellow creature of life and the experiences and satisfactions he can only realize through the living of that life takes all the possibilities he has. Only vital need and absent alternatives seem sufficient to that burden. In that lack of necessity, the presence of alternative choices, lies one significant difference between Nelson and the cultural history with which he identifies. The people of that history did not hunt to find intimacy with nature. They hunted in order to live and then embedded the necessary killing within a sacred view of life, one feature of which was belief in death's impermanence (a feature Nelson admits "abiding doubt" about).

If we do not need to hunt in order to live and there are peaceful ways to honor and participate deeply in nature's mysterious body, what remains to explain persistence of the hunt as a form of sport? Philosophers and other writers who hunt recognize a need to explain themselves and do so in many voices. I will state their case below.

Other Defenses

There seem to be three chief themes in the defense of sport hunting. One pertains to the good of the animals, another (more often unspoken than spoken) to the absence of compelling reasons *not* to kill them, and the last speaks to the good of humans. A common background assumption consists in a "realist" view of the way things are, particularly in their biological aspect. Let me begin with that.

According to this assumption, humans always have and unavoidably always will cause a certain amount of death and suffering to animals, no matter how careful we might be. Simply moving about the world doing the necessary things and minding one's own business results in collisions. Further, death is implicated in all food raising, gathering, transporting, and consuming, even for the vegetarian whose agribusiness-derived produce leaves all manner of dead birds, reptiles, and small mammals in its wake. Besides, the way of nature is that some animals eat other animals and humans have always been a part of this chain. In short, death composes a large part of the way of life. While enlightened self-interest demands prudence in human participation in that drama, only the naive imagine removing ourselves from it.

For many hunters the above serves not just as assumption but says all that needs saying. (Of course, many other hunters fail to recognize that anything needs saying at all.) Others recognize its measure of truth as germane but insufficient. After all, its appeal to accident and carelessness, to the imperatives experienced in other animals' lives, and to historically necessary behaviors cannot bear the moral weight of deliberate, unnecessary, present human action. The defense cannot rest here.

One standard argument on behalf of hunting appeals to pragmatism and utility. "Wildlife requires management" and hunting does it well, we are told. (We know that usually it is human excess and egocentrism that require the management.) Habitats are preserved that otherwise might not be, animals whose numbers tend toward excess (because of predators absent due to poorly managed humanity) are kept in check, and ecosystems and nongame animals as well benefit. These advantages arise from the direct activities of hunters in the field, from their payment of fees that end in the coffers of wildlife departments, and their activism on behalf of conservation measures to assure continued healthy numbers of game animals. One author enthuses over these benefits to the point of enshrining the dead as "martyrs" whose deaths are "sacrificial...in the best sense." (He describes the presumed benefits of the animals falling to hunters, not that they volunteered for the duty.)

So the first justification says that because hunters care enough about opportunities to shoot the animals, they care enough to invest money and influence on behalf of measures to preserve their numbers. In other words, no hunters, no dead animals, less habitat, bad management, fewer animals in the long run. The argument does not consider that a humanity advanced beyond a sport hunting stage of emotional development would be likely to find nonviolent bases for expressing its allegiance to animals and habitat.

The second justification says that, except in cases of species endangerment, no good moral reason exists *not* to kill animals. They are not persons in the philosophical sense: they lack "the essential properties of rational intelligence and autonomous will." So they can have no rights that would entail a human obligation to just let them be, to respect their need and desire to live. Arguments along these lines will point also to a host of other rights-engendering properties, but what all share is the reality that one species is constructing the case for its own priority—the one that, in early cowboy movie parlance, backs its arguments with a gun. What any of the selected properties have to do with a creature's wish to live and to experience the unique goods of that life remains mysterious.

The third defense asserts the good life for humans, a prominent aspect of which, hunters say, consists in the experience of hunting. To begin with, hunting is perhaps instinctive and in any event natural to our species due to original necessity. As an essential human trait it yearns for expression; to thwart it may be to diminish our possibilities for fulfillment. Evolution has led to occasions for the exercise of human skill, in this case the development of excellence in the predatory arts. In hunting one engages most intimately with nature in its depth and mystery, its inherent dramas of conflict and serenity, death and life. The hunter sees the eyes of his dinner, you could say, an act most honest in modern, technologically cushioned times. In the killing and in the rituals and traditions of the hunt he experiences and expresses a reverence for sacred nature unknown to most nonhunters. In sum, authentic being and authentic participation open themselves to the hunter, vividly and incomparably.

Challenging the Defenses

Where are the animals midst all these arguments? They are not merely mute, but as more than symbol and object for imaginative manipulation, they are absent. We hear a sort of species solipsism, a monological voice. The ongoing conversation with the other experienced by the ancients and the few remaining traditionals in their daily intercourse with earth/spirit has gone missing, as it must in the absence of a mutuality that hears as well as speaks.

What can mutuality mean between human and other animals? For some it means a more expansive experiencing, much of it virtually indescribable but sometimes eloquent with empathy and responsiveness. Much about animals we cannot know, but we can be present and wonder deeply. David Romtvedt puts it nicely: "Not knowing what an animal's experience of its life is, I am reluctant to accept that we may without consequence shorten those lives. Life wants to live." It does; we can see that.

Defenders of hunting sometimes acknowledge ambivalence. Said one, "The thrill of the kill is often followed by twinges of guilt." Seven years later this hunter, Ann Causey, still frets: "How can anyone both revere life and seek to extinguish it in pursuit of recreation?" She frets but continues to hunt, and as best I can tell still has not answered the question adequately.

Defenders are amid serious contradiction, it seems to me. For example, Ted Kerasote, a thoughtful hunter if ever one was, appeals to hunting's ancient, honorable origins as he sadly views modern hunter shortcomings. He wants it recreated as "sacred activity" in which "kindness, compassion, and sympathy for those other species" have their essential parts. Hunters must resurrect, he says, "older principles of mutual regard between species" and the "reverence and humility" to recognize that killing "can only be done for good reasons." In this manner, hunting can remain "one of our important and fundamental weddings with nature." What do words mean when used in these ways, in the domain of sport killing?

To speak of weddings speaks of connectedness of the most profound sort. If, for example, someone tells you he killed his spouse, that he gave her a narcotic cocktail so potent as to still her heart, you will wonder at the meaning of this. A history of infidelity and large insurance policies of which he is the beneficiary suggests one possibility. But if you know instead that she had an incurable disease with unrelenting pain and physical humiliations, that she had always spoken of her deep wish never to be required to endure such insults, and that they were devoted to one another and had a prior agreement, then you recognize eutha-

nasia and know it reflects their connectedness and respectful doing for the other. Some deaths connect us with life's
values while some fragment and offend them.

Even when we think of a communion of life where it makes
sense to experience animals' deaths as a gift of nurture—
situations of necessity—we cannot doubt how they would
feel about life taken for sport. Animals' experience of life
may remain ultimately unknowable to us, but can we seriously question that in their way they value it? The creatures
cling to existence, after all.

Some speak of the spirituality and reverence of the hunt.
They have the highest regard for their prey, they say, and
experience something spiritual in the stalk and shoot. I try
to think of some other dimension in which one could speak
sensibly of intentional and unnecessary extirpation of something whose existence he highly values. Nothing comes to
mind. Elsewhere when such momentous choices are made
we justify with vital need, an absence of alternatives. Where
do we say that the best way to express reverence is through
willed destruction of the revered?

Spiritual masters have been consistent about this: the
more of self, the less of spirit. Self-forgetting, they urge as
the path. One does not seek spiritual experience to enhance
selfhood, to self-actualize, as it is called. One has the experience because he receptively hears the address and recognizes its self-transcending validity and ultimacy. He yields
to it. Ethics works similarly and in concord to restrain "the
fat, relentless ego," as Iris Murdoch called it. Self-seeking
helps to create imperialisms and dominations and as sure
as anything kills spiritual realization in its crib.

Self- and human-centeredness. Elevation of self, depre-
ciation of other. Human conversation once included the elements, fellow plant and animal beings, the mystery: all re-
ciprocally spoke and were heard. Now we mostly talk to ourselves, and a valuational assumption accompanies the
change. The other loses the quality of independent value
and diminishes to the state of diversion, resource, impediment, or commodity for use and disposal. Animals over-
whelmingly appear to us as food. A hunter in "Gooseberry
Marsh" explains her predilection this way: "Because I want

this kind of intimate relationship with the food I eat." She thinks, rightly, that factory-farmed animals are obscenely objectified. But I think of the ducks she wounded and lost or blasted asunder on the way to her dinner, and of Nelson's deer: one moment alert, muscles tensed, standing in beauty, and then a shot and the buck drops and is hung, bled, eviscerated, flayed, dismembered, and laid on the fire. The hunter's kill has more dignity than the disfigured industrial creature yet still has died to satisfy a taste, only a preference.

The author/hunter in the Marsh reveals more than she intends. In a six-line paragraph about a feast she uses the words "we" and "our" nine times. A few column inches later twenty-two lines contain twenty-one self-referential pronouns: we, our, me, etc. She closes the article in this fashion: "Can *I* have a relationship with these animals alive? Or is the killing, the eating, that magical bridging, a crucial part of *my* love, part of *my* relationship with these animals, with the world? What does it mean that in *my* body, helping to keep *me* alive, to make *me* joyful, to share joy with people *I* love, is the breast of a greenhead mallard that *I* shot down on a cool autumn day and scooped from the cold water with *my* hand?" (Italics are mine.) As the language, however idealized, reveals part of the meaning is self-absorption, a preoccupation with her own desires that easily trumps the interests of others, even the vital interest to retain their lives.

Individuals are responsible for making these choices, but the full story implicates the culture in setting the terms for choosing. Kerasote aptly describes hunter values and actions that embarrass him as being consistent with other culturally sanctioned "dominionistic" activities such as developer destruction of wetlands, agribusiness, factory farming, clear-cut forests. "All the accusations that may be fairly leveled against the American hunter—greedy, thoughtless, lazy, consumptive, sexist—can also be brought against our culture at large." He intends to explain rather than excuse, to portray hunters as representative of the population as a whole, to broaden the context. I would broaden it even more. Not only the "slob" hunter expresses much that is unfortunately tolerated within the culture. "Ethical" hunters as

THE SPORT OF HUNTING

well—self-restrained, thoughtful, respectful, nature-loving folks that they are—continue the Western tradition of human separation from and elevation above other existence such that unnecessary killing has little sting but much glorification. The separated self feels entitled.

How should we properly stand toward the *others* within nature? We have clues but assign them categories for dismissal: mere emotion, sentimentality, romanticism, naivete, anthropomorphism. My wife and I found ourselves in the midst of an exemplary clue, one many have experienced but for us the first time. A fallen nestling, soon followed by another, perhaps his sibling, appeared one day. Grackles. They are common in this part of the world and mostly disdained as "nuisance birds." On scales of beauty and euphony these two were off the chart. They ate much and seemingly defecated more, but hourly or thereabouts we fed them and cleaned them and found ourselves worrying about them. They engaged our attention and our care.

What did that mean? I think the responsiveness engendered by these birds went beyond their obvious need for help. Their simple being as grackles nudged its way into our arena of concern and respect. They existed; they loudly yearned to live; they affected us and demanded a place at the table of existence. We could do nothing but honor that.

Perhaps such honoring and engagement with the lives around us is truer to the Good and the natural reality of our relations with them than any other response. Analogous to tin-eared oblivion at a symphony, if we miss that it may be due to what's missing in us rather than them.

Hints of the impact of a heightened feeling for the lives of other-than-human animals appeared in Nelson shortly before he shot the buck. When he first saw him Nelson was downwind and concealed so the animal slowly approached him unaware. "He comes so quickly that I have no chance to shoot, and then he is so close I haven't the heart to do it." A paragraph later, "In the Koyukon way, he has come to me; but in my own he has come too close." Only when the buck finally sees him and flees is he "freed of the ambiguities that held me before," and he shoots the animal.

The buck's flight after coming so near raises an obvious

question about his readiness to "give" himself to the hunter, but that does not concern me here. Why did his physical proximity to Nelson neutralize his capacity to kill? Is it possible that when an animal becomes real to us, as closeness, knowledge, and attentiveness to his individual being tends to promote, he becomes too real to kill in good conscience?

I respect the desire expressed by some hunters for intimacy with the animals and nature. Many people's experience confirms that our times of deep engagement with the natural world provide unique entry into substantial existence. But shouldn't the hunter reconsider a form of engagement that negates lives. Perhaps the reverence sought in hunting can be better found in encounters that affirm the other's equal need and desire to live, rather than those that kill for no better reason than sport.

REFERENCES

Causey, Ann S. "On the Morality of Hunting." *Environmental Ethics*, Vol. 11, No. 4 (Winter 1989), pp. 327-343.

Dominico, Terry & Mark Newman. *Bears of the World.* New York: Facts On File, 1988.

Leggett, Mike. "Spoilsports try to ruin a sick boy's dream wish." *Austin American-Statesman*, May 16, 1996.

Loftin, Robert W. "The Morality of Hunting." *Environmental Ethics*, Vol. 6, No. 3 (Fall 1984), pp. 241-250.

McCarthy, Cormac. *The Crossing.* New York: Vintage Books, 1994.

Nelson, Richard. *The Island Within.* San Francisco: North Point Press, 1989.

ORION, Winter 1996:

Kerasote, Ted. "To Preserve the Hunt," pp.13-19.
Romtvedt, David. "Strange Communion," pp. 20-24.
Causey, Ann S. "What's the Problem with Hunting?," pp. 25-28.

Legler, Gretchen. "Gooseberry Marsh," pp. 29-33.

Rennicke, Jeff. *Bears of Alaska in Life and Legend.* Boulder: Roberts Rinehart, Inc., 1987.

Thoreau, Henry David. *The Maine Woods.* New York: Harper & Row, 1987.

Vitali, Theodore R. "Sport Hunting: Moral or Immoral?" *Environmental Ethics,* Vol. 12, No. 1 (Spring 1990), pp. 69-82.

8

EXPERIMENTING ON ANIMALS

Imagine, if you can, what could lead you deliberately to impose torment and misery into the life of another: a dog or a cat, a baboon or a rhesus monkey, a mouse or a bird or a rabbit. And not just this day and this creature but as part of an enterprise that works year around imposing its suffering on perhaps 50,000,000 up to 100,000,000 animals in the United States and five or ten times that number around the world.

What could lead you to do these things: inject, insert, infuse the animals with drugs, poisons, and other toxic substances; deprive them of sleep, food, and water; irradiate and electroshock their bodies; cut into living brains and sever spinal cords; smash heads with blunt, heavy objects; fire bullets through them; implant electrodes; blind, deafen, and silence them; overheat or undercool their bodies; asphyxiate, bleed, and maim; deprive infants of contact with mothers and isolate adults; stress, frighten, and foment anxiety? And then kill them.

What could lead you to do any of this? You are not necessarily consumed with ambition or a relentless pursuit of profits. Neither are you psychopathically cruel, seized with a will to power, or deeply divided emotionally and thus desensitized. You would need very good reasons to assume the moral burden of such deplorable actions. Performing these procedures, which so profoundly injure individuals as well as the moral texture of culture itself, would seem to require a purpose of the loftiest nature. But would such a good purpose tolerate such measures for its accomplishment?

Biomedical experimentation on animals is a well-established, well-defended, and well-challenged endeavor. My interest comes to this: what view of humankind and of its fundamental relation with its cohabitants on Earth fosters and permits such behavior? For an answer we look toward a form of vanity, at how woven into human conceptions the notion has become of humanity as the crown of creation, that which all else exists only to serve. Some medical experimenters believe, based on that self-elevation, that their actions need involve little or any moral concern for the animals' lives. Others, however, recognize moral complexity and feel for the victims, and it is those who are of interest here.

In the United Kingdom in 1986, following passage of the "Animals (Scientific Procedures) Act 1986," the Institute of Medical Ethics established a Working Party of scientists, physicians, philosophers, animal welfarists, and others to study ethical issues in biomedical research using animals. The result in 1991 was a book: *Lives in the Balance: The Ethics of Using Animals in Biomedical Research.* I use it as text for this discussion because it represents a good example of pro-researchers trying to be sensitive to the plight and fate of their research subjects (objects). Like a preacher's sin, therefore, their human-centeredness stands out all the more poignantly.

Necessity

Necessity sometimes mothers invention; at others it fathers justification. A large part of the defense for sacrificing animals to biomedical experimentation relies on its presumed necessity relative to both means and ends; that is, there is no better way to meet essential human needs for prevention and treatment of disease and dysfunction. Alternatives to animals (for example, mathematical and computer modeling, cell and tissue cultures, epidemiology) have been much discussed. Rather than enter that area I will say only that, on the one hand, if habit, territoriality, and complacency were set aside and more efforts were made to find alternatives, one can hardly doubt that legions of animals could be freed from their laboratory shackles. But on the other hand, for some research purposes they could not be, and since I intend to make a case for unconditional abolition regardless, I will focus on these cases where no better way exists at this time to empirically test a concoction or treatment or hypothesis. In these situations the researcher believes that he merely concedes to necessity on behalf of the greater good.

The Institute's Working Party addressed this question of alternatives and reported that they would welcome any that were "at least as satisfactory as the use of animals for the relevant scientific purposes." They were unclear where the burden of proof on this matter lay, but in tone it sounds like the opposition's, and a heavy burden indeed. For if an alternative were a bit more expensive or time-consuming or troublesome to implement, it would not satisfy this reservation. The Working Party explains twice that it is only "a hypothetical historical question" and therefore unanswerable whether gains accomplished on the bodies of animals could have been achieved in other ways, and the past cannot be changed anyway. They also recognize that we are not in an emergency situation. Raging epidemics do not decimate populations, but essential human needs remain nonetheless. Further, they acknowledge that human behavior (those things we do to ourselves in how we choose to live and what we put into our bodies) causes a number of serious human ailments, but they are resigned that "there are formidable difficulties in persuading people to change their sexual, dietary and other customary forms of behaviour." In short, the Working Party hopes for alternatives but believes there is a host of human medical needs and desires that cannot be satisfied without animal research.

Those "formidable difficulties" in changing people's (including researchers) customary ways deserve some thought. The Party seems to say that due to human self-indulgence, weakness, obstinacy, and lack of operative intelligence "lower" animals must be tormented and killed to save us from ourselves. That seems a strange notion, but even regarding largely non-self-induced disorders, where does the idea come from that humans have a necessity for (a fundamental right to) relief? A wish or a want or even a need is understandable, but an obligation, a necessity, does not naturally follow. Do we also have a right to be born beautiful and brilliant and physically sound, of sterling parentage and happy as larks? Are we owed an escape from the contingencies of existence that make some people sick and some die young? Where does this kind of thinking come from and where does it end?

With ever-increasing clarity we see this "human desires first!" mythology growing in the midst of a diminishing natural world and a metastasizing industrial domain. We certainly see it within the laboratory. The insinuating corrosiveness and momentum of this world view continues. The Party understands that some animal-exploiting research involves rather minor disorders or ones affecting very few people, and that this might seem problematic given the unsavory consequences for the animals. But they reason that unforeseen or accidental benefits may appear and "respect for the autonomy and feelings of those suffering from conditions of the kind described" establish a moral claim to forge onward. Indeed, they say that such quibbling about the severity of the disorder merely indulges "crude quantitative or qualitative utilitarian" considerations. This is an odd allegation since central to the Animals Act is the instruction, before permitting an experiment, to "weigh the likely adverse effects on the animals concerned against the benefit likely to accrue as a result of the [research] programme." When some creatures are used as "a means only" to other creatures' ends, utilitarianism is insufficient moral philosophy. But even so, it requires consistency in the application; if utility serves to justify animal sacrifice on the altar of great benefits, ought it not spare the animals' agony when the scales tilt the other direction?

The Working Party's dexterity shows itself similarly around the question of testing what some consider trivial products (such as cosmetics or yet another cleanser) at the expense of animals. They appeal to "public demand" and "size of the market" and "legitimate demand" for the products as indicators of nontriviality. "'Triviality' issues are too uncertain and too complex," they explain, and "the judgement is best made by the consumers of such products." The animals lose again.

The Party argues that a necessity defense derives from the Common Law doctrine that the normally unacceptable becomes acceptable when it is "the only way of achieving a greater and lawful benefit"; for example, shooting a hijacker to save passengers. In ethics and law, they say, two things must be shown: "(1) that the evil prevented is greater than that done; and (2) that there is no less drastic method of achieving the stated aim." Based on this, a scientist "is required morally to demonstrate at least four things: (1) that the goal is worthwhile; (2) that it has a high moral claim to be achieved; (3) that there is no less drastic method of achieving it; and (4) that there actually is some reasonable possibility of the project achieving the goal." The striking feature in this moral algorithm is that in the move from ethics and law to science the standards increase numerically (from two to four) while decreasing substantively. The "evil prevented" (for humans) remains in the picture, but what happened to weighing the "evil done" (to animals)? It vanished. We are left with a postulated necessity due to absent alternatives and essential needs, but the ethical weight of the deeds done to the animal subjects of research falls from consideration. Worse, what began in the hijacking scenario as the killing of aggressors to save victims becomes now killing victims to save their aggressors. The animals have become, in Carol Adams' phrase, "absent referents." Such is the power of human-centeredness to narrow the frame of reference. The playing field tilts drastically in favor of those who write the rules.

Assuming the priority of human over all other goods has a potent pervasiveness. So potent is it that the Party moves the necessity of biomedical experimentation on animals onward into another dimension: such research becomes not just a necessary means toward vital ends, but mandatory. Thus, "the moral community's commitment to the common and individual good appears to have been more adequately expressed by the use of animals than it would have been by not using them." Also, they announce, "there may in fact be a moral requirement that the animal procedures should be carried out." One can hardly overestimate the intensity of humanity's self-interestedness.

Another example appears in the pursuit of scientific knowledge that lacks apparent therapeutic or practical benefits. Once again, "any significant advance in scientific knowledge is an inherent good, and may serve as a justification for using animals to that end." The inherent good of life, that of the creature in the cage, again goes absent. While some consider *this* good, the inherent good of a life preserved, one of the most fundamental of goods, it will not survive a contest with human desire.

The idea of medicine's moral mandate to seek cures by all means has been examined at length by the medical ethicist Daniel Callahan. He believes that modern medicine's ambition has become to banish mortality: "It has declared war on death, on the ravages of time, and most of all on the nature that brings them about." In its research and clinical agendas it has come "to look upon death as a correctable biological deficiency." Medicine arrived at this position through pride, complicity with patients' fantasies, and a distorted "moral logic" that emerged as it increased its effectiveness in treating illness, allowing it, oddly, to challenge the naturalness of death. Callahan explains that this moral dimension "soon took the form of a simple principle: since death is an evil in human life, we have a moral obligation to use medical means to combat it. What can be done to struggle against death ought to be done." In short, an expansive sense of the sanctity of human life merged with the hubris of scientific progress and resulted in the removal of humanity from nature: "The transformation of death from a biological evil to a moral evil as well had been effected." Humanity would strive to assume nature's responsibility for death.

The unfortunate results of this moralization of illness and death are apparent in distorted medical-societal priorities: an immense mushrooming of the techno-medical enterprise; deep confusion about death's place in life; exacerbation of human alienation from nature; and the common pathos of dying prolonged technologically beyond life's desire. Callahan suggests we recover a more realistic sense of ourself and of medicine as a human-sized endeavor rather than "a holy one." We can begin by accepting constraints on our dreams: "The social constraint on the self means that its desire for health and its desire to avoid death do not impose ruinous burdens on others, whether family members or the public [or, I add, experimental subjects]....The personal constraint should be the grounding of the self in an understanding of human nature that grasps and takes seriously a fundamental reality: to be human is to be mortal."

And fallible. Western culture is rarely friendly toward ideas of self-restraint. Its guiding ideals—growth, progress, acquisitiveness—will find no comfort with such heresy. But it sometimes helps to remind ourselves of the wisdom we impart to our children: there are legal, moral, civil, and personal limits in a responsible life.

Comparative Moral Status

The purpose here is to examine animal-based biomedical experimentation in terms of how it expresses humanity's sense of its place in the universe. We have seen several forms of the assumption of unwavering human priority within the great scheme of things. Near the conclusion of the Working Party's report they finally specify the differentiated categories of existence occupied by humans and all other creatures that justifies instrumental utilization of the latter by humans. That perspective merits a close look.

The defense of using animals in this way stands on three legs: great potential benefit, necessary evil, and the lower moral status of nonhumans. While the benefits undoubtedly are exaggerated, it would not be honest to deny their existence. Even if they accrued to very few people, the Working Party claims that the good for these humans sufficiently compensates for the evil means.

The argument that the achievement of those benefits for humans absolutely must occur has been challenged above. Food, water, air: these are necessities. Cure or prevention of human ailments (most of which are at least partially self-inflicted) represents a preoccupying anxiety (and major growth industry) whose alleviation would be desirable—extremely so in many cases. The search for causes and efficacious responses surely seems laudable, but need and necessity are significantly different categories. If it were truly a necessity, would not the Working Party have been compelled to acknowledge the rightness of occasionally using nonvoluntary human experimental subjects? Humans unfortunately have come to the conclusion that whatever we want we should have, at whatever cost to other-than-human existence. While some may experience that want as a compelling necessity, vain wish does not make it so.

The third leg of the argument for animal experimentation cites their inferior moral status. This is probably the most vital one, for no matter how powerful the need nor how great the intended benefit, without inferiority no moral ground exists to use human and nonhuman in different ways. And with inferiority presumed, neither the need nor the benefit must prove itself so decisively as it would otherwise.

The Party begins with a discussion of the ethics of using human subjects, sees this governed by the requirements of informed consent from the subjects and the intent not to harm by the researchers, and concludes that humans are inviolable. In other words, any risks occasioned to a human must be impersonally assigned, individualized, reasonable, and justifiable and acceptable to him or her. This composes the notion of deep respect for inherent good, and it is a vital principle.

The animals lack this good, according to the Party. In particular, they are inferior because they lack self-consciousness and rationality. Humans have an "enduring self," an awareness of past and future as well as present, an ability to abstract and symbolize and to think and plan and to talk about these things. With all this, the experience of suffering and the prospect of death have for us a unique poignancy and harm, for we may relate them to our personal identities—knowing about them makes them worse than simply living them.

These considerations about human nature ring with a truth that their postulation as the ground of superior moral worth does not echo. My awareness of impending death adds bite to the event, yet I would not give up that awareness even if I could, so perhaps its poignancy has rewards. We are gifted with a capacity to reflect on our life's course; if that adds harmful bite at times, is it not compensated by the gift's largess? Aren't all the "harms" that are supposed to derive from our remarkable capacities more than compensated by the deep satisfactions those capacities allow? In short, the argument is self-serving in much the same way as arguing that people who are poor or of relatively low intelligence should be the ones sent off to war, for after all, they have less to lose.

Even so, we can acknowledge that the suffering and death of a human are sometimes evil and always painful, and the inherent good that his or her life composes should be sufficient to prohibit the deliberate infliction of harms. Good and sufficient reasons clearly exist not to experiment on unwilling humans.

But do reasons to avoid harm of my neighbor on one side release me to impose harm to my neighbor on the other? The Working Party helps us see some of what makes wrong an avoidable choice to hurt humans. They do not show that other kinds of concern would not make equally wrong those hurts inflicted on nonhumans. Their assumption that the research enterprise comprises moral mandate—that it must go on, the only choice being which creature will be its experimental subject—may preclude recognition of such concerns. But what if we saw *life*, rather than this or that *expression of life*, as the great good? What can we know about the kinds of nonrational satisfaction and value the animal finds in living, or the kinds of nonreflective terror and loss the manipulated animal finds in the laboratory? All healthy animals, human and nonhuman, experience the good of being and strive to hold on to it.

The chief thing that all we animals have is the capacity for direct experience, to fulfill a life course. We humans experience and then *reflect* upon it, but experience is primary. If I tell you of my joy in the mountains you will see that the being there mattered more than the report. Not that the capacity to share and reflect on the experience is without value. The sharing consummates and extends the experience and is part of what makes our way special for us. But who can demonstrate that the ability to reflect has greater overall value in the grand scheme? Picture existence not as a hierarchy of betters over inferiors but as a sphere on which all life forms go their interesting and intersecting ways equidistant from the center. When you contemplate your own death (or grieve a cherished one who already has died), do you hurt for lost rationality and self-consciousness, or for the transit out of being into nothing? Why have spiritually wise ones always urged selfless presence within immediate experience as having priority over cogitative activity? Although the uses to which we put it are a decidedly mixed bag, we are good at our kind of thinking and as a result may think too much of it.

Reflective people who exploit animals justify themselves with a common rehearsal of differences between them and us. The differences to some extent are real, but in the absence of real necessity are of little relevance to moral value and choice. Absent necessity, why would anyone want to judge the relative value of lives? If several of us are together and one begins asserting his superiority, the rest might move away. He propounds the stuff of narcissism, racism, fascism; we do not want that. As we face necessity (which we rarely do in this way), listing differences may help with the tragic choice between one life and another. Unless we simply cast lots we are forced to find some criteria for the choice, and range of experiencing and consciousness and all the rest of the inventory may provide direction and weight. But when the contenders are all human, it's a choice we try to escape, as we should whoever the contenders.

Sometimes the rehearsal of differences fails to fully justify the determined researcher. This is the case when he sees humans lacking the cherished qualities—infants, the senile, or mentally handicapped. The researcher backs away knowing he would not subject them to his protocols. The Working Party has a way out of this dilemma. While granting that membership in the human species cannot be a *necessary* condition for higher moral status (savant chimpanzees or extra-terrestrials could pass the test), they affirm that membership provides a *sufficient* condition. Though underdeveloped or permanently impaired the humans indicated above "possess ... *the nature of a rational self-conscious creature*" (italics are the Party's) and so may be "awarded" the status. I can find no meaning for "nature" in this context other than "membership," and that reveals that justificatory argument has expired and been replaced with predetermined ascription of status. A creature need not be human for enhanced moral entitlement (only human-like in the designated qualities) but being any kind of human (however defective in whatever ways) will gain one entry.

The dice are loaded and the deck is stacked—that cannot surprise us. The powerful find it hard to relinquish any ground of perceived self-interest. Human-centered mystification (that background assumption that suffuses thought: a universe tailor-made and custom-built for man's delight alone) has a self-gratifying potency very hard to escape. The Working Party trimmed the assumption's edges on behalf of increased "humanity" in research, but its dominant convictions survived.

When parents look at their child they recognize that their superiority has granted them a privilege and a responsibility. The privilege of being there with that child, the responsibility of tending and protecting, of doing no harm. The same recognition but more remote accompanies their view of children not their own. Greater capacities in certain areas are their own good with their own pleasures and responsibilities, but no ticket to abuse the weaker—whoever the weaker might be.

What would happen if tomorrow animal exploitation in biomedical research ended, never to be resumed? Researchers undoubtedly would announce impending doom; research, after all, is an arm of progress and shares its momentum and self-justifications. What *can* be done *must* be done, because it can be done (profitably). More realistically, some knowledge and new medical interventions might be delayed and perhaps in a few cases precluded, at least for the near future. The research industry would not know as much or do as much as quickly as it would prefer, but life would go on. Would it be less favorable life, all things considered?

If you believe that the best route to healthful living runs through doctors' offices, hospitals, and pharmacies—that treating illness founds health—you might face the prospect with fear and dismay. Even wounded pride if, with the Working Party, you consider that "enhanced concern for animal welfare...[means] lowering the moral status of human beings and the strength of our obligations to humanity." (Did enhanced concern for black slaves have this morally lowering effect in obligations toward white people?) On the other hand, if your concern for animals means raising their status and our obligations to them without in the least lowering anything toward humans, you will have a more benign and optimistic view of the prospect. You will even be intrigued as you realize that a change of this magnitude could not occur in isolation.

A decision to respect the moral inviolability of all animals, as was granted to only human animals formerly, would reflect an utterly different view of the human place in the cosmos. Rather than separating from and objectifying other existence, we would have regained the experience of connectedness. And we would attain a measure of receptive care and respect toward the community that conceived and supports us. Further, a humanity that refused to relieve its suffering by imposing it on others would be a humanity that would not accept the coarsening, aggressive, and fragmented society that ours increasingly is. It would organize itself around answering questions about the real good for persons, families, and communities rather than indenturing itself to the purported good of techno-consumerist monomania and *Homo sapien* elitism. And if the studies regarding environmentally induced illness, stress-induced illness, illness from anxiety and depression and the assorted forms of chemical and behavioral self-treatment and acting-out are as credible as they appear, if respect for life spread and so reduced these, then it would be a far healthier humanity after all.

Pie-in-the-sky, perhaps, but food for thought. How much of the societal and commercial/industrial pathology that increasingly afflict us arises in the space that has been made to separate us from other living things? Our alienation from animals and nature and their perception as primarily resources does not stop with them. It extends itself to relations among our own kind. Lives sacrificed emotionally and

spiritually to corporate profitability and work and materialist aspiration, urban mayhem, young people killing themselves and each other at alarming and escalating rates, the
generalized readiness to rely on aggression to accomplish
one's ends—the litany is familiar. Self-interested preoccu-
pations run wild and they require, in order to run, the empty
space created of detachment, its occupation by monetary
(and medical) goods, and the vision of all *otherness* as mainly
grist for one's mill, resource for one's desires.

So if the lab cages were empty tomorrow? To accept limits on medical research is not to embrace death and suffering. But honor in this realm has a dual character: courageous resolve to prolong life and relieve suffering combined
with the wisdom of finitude, the readiness to accept reality
and ethical constraint. Death and suffering are part of the
human condition, and there are biological and moral limits
to the struggle against them. When the struggle becomes
unbounded, the struggler is morally diminished. An unworthy life surpasses suffering in unacceptability. There is no
moral necessity to make humans feel better and live longer,
through any and all methods. Without moral embeddedness
the struggle will fail our deeper possibilities, even when it
succeeds on its own terms.

REFERENCES

Adams, Carol. *The Sexual Politics of Meat.* New York:
Continuum, 1990.

Callahan, Daniel. *The Troubled Dream of Life.* New York:
Simon & Schuster, 1993.

Smith, Jane A. & Kenneth M. Boyd (eds.). *Lives in the
Balance: The Ethics of Using Animals in Biomedical Research.*
Oxford: Oxford University Press, 1991.

9

ANOTHER LOOK AT THE "PATHETIC FALLACY"

> Nature and human life are as various as our several con-
> stitutions. Who shall say what prospect life offers to an-
> other? Could a greater miracle take place than for us to
> look through each other's eyes for an instant? We should
> live in all the ages of the world in an hour; ay, in all the
> worlds of the ages.
>
> Thoreau, *Walden*

One thread connecting these essays has been the discernment of difference and similarity between humankind
and the rest of animalkind. And then to ask, what difference
do the differences make? What respect do we owe these other-
than-humans? How can we characterize a right relationship with them? Though I think it should not, the response
to the question of respect is usually based on the perception, and in particular the evaluation, of differences. When
these are considered morally compelling (to the detriment of
the other-than-humans), we hear the voice of the
anthropocentrist. One of the more extreme speakers in this
voice was Francis Bacon: "Man, if we look to final causes,
may be regarded as the centre of the world, insomuch that if
man were taken away from the world, the rest would seem
to be all astray, without aim or purpose."

Those, on the other hand, who emphasize commonality
and identification between other animals and us are accused
of anthropomorphism—the attribution of human character-

istics to other animals. In 1856 John Ruskin coined a phrase that has become associated with it—"the pathetic fallacy." Timeworn, it remains with us yet and is capacious enough in its current uses to reject identifications between humans and all the rest of nature. Ruskin's wrestling with this phenomenon in the variety of its aspects makes for an interesting story.

At the outset I must say that Ruskin was not always consistent or clear in his discussion of the fallacy, and as I do not pretend being a Ruskin scholar, my purpose is to use him illustratively rather than to track his attitudes toward the notion. His primary concern was the fallacy's contamination of poetry and other arts. Mine relates to its assumptions and uses and to the kinds of experiences humans have with nature and animals that the fallacy's indictment has been leveled against. For if we accept the indictment, we accept that humans and the living world that gave us birth have somehow come to occupy exceedingly different realms of existence—with drastically different ethical substance and value.

The Pathetic Fallacy

Who are we looking at when we look at animals? What do we look to find?

The ire that drove Ruskin to write the essay "Of the Pathetic Fallacy" (within his collection *Modern Painters, Vol. III*)arose in response to certain "metaphysicians" who, in his view, had misconstrued the relationship between sensory input and external reality. Observing that "subjective" experiences such as taste and color depended on a perceptive organ (a tongue, an eye) for realization, many of these philosophers erroneously went on "to a farther opinion, that it does not much matter what things are in themselves, but only what they are to us; and that the only real truth of them is their appearance to, or effect upon, us." He responded that "the power of producing" sensation resided in the thing perceived, regardless of human presence or absence. "And, therefore, the gentian and the sky are always verily blue, whatever philosophy may say to the contrary; and if you do not see them blue when you look at them, it is not their fault, but yours." The metaphysicians' error in this was not itself the pathetic fallacy, but Ruskin implied that their confusion about human perception and the reality of things contributed to the fallacy's prevalence.

His concern in this was to differentiate true from false experiences as they were presented, for example, in poetry. "All violent [i.e., intense] feelings have the same effect. They produce in us a falseness in all our impressions of external things, which I would generally characterize as the 'pathetic fallacy.'" Poetic locutions such as "The spendthrift crocus," "The cruel, crawling foam" (of the sea), and "The one red leaf, the last of its clan,/That dances as often as dance it can," illustrated the fallacy in practice. He approved of metaphor that expressed true feeling and which maintained the distinction between "pure fact" and imagination, but condemned insincere expression or false impression (that is, "appearances...entirely unconnected with any real power or character in the object, and only imputed to it by us."). In short, "the spirit of truth must guide us."

Finally, Ruskin addressed himself not only to true appearances but to the person who encountered them. Both those who had right perception without feeling and those with exorbitant feeling but poor perception were at the bottom of his ranking. At the top were those "who feel strongly, think strongly, and see truly (first order of poets); and the men who, strong as human creatures can be, are yet submitted to influences stronger than they, and see in a sort untruly, because what they see is inconceivably above them. This last is the usual condition of prophetic inspiration."

Two things to emphasize about these superior persons: the "governance" of clear sight and hard thinking by no means precludes passion, imagination, vision, or richly associative experience of things; and second, "it would be inhuman and monstrous" not to be powerfully moved by powerful external influences, even mysterious ones (such as the sense of "Divine presence"). In other words, Ruskin's conception of fact and truth is a commodious one. His concern simply was to preserve the clarity of real distinctions and between true and false appearance, and not to deny nature's richness and mystery. Of one poet characterized by animated descriptions of nature he said approvingly, "instead of making Nature anywise subordinate to himself, he makes himself subordinate to her—follows her lead simply—does not venture to bring his own cares and thoughts into her pure and quiet presence—paints her in her simple and universal truth, adding no result of momentary passion or fancy." The pathetic fallacy, it seems, is a more complicated notion than many of its modern usages as aspersion have reflected, for it can reside in missing the real as well as in projecting the unreal.

Ruskin, then, bestirred himself against artists who would confuse what was self with what was other. Today one said to be guilty of the pathetic fallacy, as often as not, is someone who speaks of animals as creatures who have more than simple rote lives, lives scripted biologically for the most constricted forms of being. Such "romantic sentimentalists" are said to project *human* qualities on to the animals, qualities they do not possess. But if they have inner qualities, such as thoughts, feelings, and intentions (like humans in some manner), how can we discover it?

Anthropomorphism

Where Ruskin strove to disabuse artists of false impression and expression, others in our time seek to provide the same service to and through scientists. According to these anti-anthropomorphists (the British ethologist John Kennedy, for example), we cannot assume, assert, or deny that animals have conscious experience. There is no compelling evidence either way. But in fact the belief in such consciousness cannot possibly "meet the normal scientific requirement for proof," "it cannot be tested," and so is not even a scientific hypothesis. Nonetheless, he says that as a working hypothesis "anthropomorphism [thinking one perceives animal consciousness] is treated here as a definite mistake."

This conviction leads to assertions that have a strange sound to them. Where I sometimes notice (or think I do) that my dog tries to get my attention or to anticipate whether we will jog west or east at the intersection this morning, Kennedy admonishes that "To assume that an animal is trying to do something is unwarranted anthropomorphism,....it is natural selection and not the animal that ensures that what it does mostly 'makes sense.'" Quoting another investigator (G.G. Gallup), he wants us to realize that animals "'have evolved in many instances to act as if they had minds.'" They behave in ways we might expect them to if they were conscious, "But the beliefs and desires of animals remain purely metaphorical."

Kennedy recognizes that for some scientists the lack of acceptable evidence for animal consciousness leads to personal dilemmas, specifically around the question of animal suffering. In other words, some people who study animal behavior or biology as professional scientists also *care* about animals and find it difficult, in the nonscientist aspects of themselves, to doubt that they experience states like pain or suffering. But Kennedy remains adamant: "We can attain an empathic 'understanding' of an animal's feelings, but not a scientific understanding of them; we have no scientific knowledge that it has any." (Since, as described in earlier essays, animal welfarists justify their killing of animals on the grounds of preventing and alleviating suffering, they may find this alarming.) So to perceive as suffering animal experiences that seem unambiguous to so many—hunger, abandonment, abuse, experimentation, the gross mobility restrictions and manipulations down on the factory farm—falls into the error of anthropomorphism.

The preceding quotation from Kennedy deserves a second look. Science transformed into *scientism* we know to be the elevation of a scientific world view or method to a dominating, all-encompassing status in relation to other ways of knowing. It is suggestive of a person with two good legs who insists on getting about on only one, which he chooses for unknown reasons to favor. Hopping has its uses, but why choose self-limitation in lieu of the balance and grace of two legs walking, running, sometimes dancing in tandem? The use of quotation marks with "understanding" associated with empathy toward animals but not when conjoined with science, as he does, is to tell us that the underutilized leg, even when tentatively brought to the ground, cannot be truly relied upon, for it is too insubstantial, "metaphorical," "untestable." But empathic understanding represents the knowledge and comprehension that one derives from attentive observation, participating in relationship, and imaginatively taking the place of another. I do not know how one could live maturely without engaging in and crediting empathy, unscientific though it must be, for lives are not lived within laboratories. For the thoroughgoing anti-anthropomorphist, though, this will not do. Kennedy acknowledges that most ethological field workers, those with the closest direct experience with animals, do not doubt animal consciousness. Mere intuition, he scoffs, "by itself [it] is regarded as unacceptably anthropomorphic." Valuable as science unquestionably can be, here the scientist walks on one leg only.

I want to challenge the dismissal as anthropomorphism of claims for an independent and value-laden essence inherent in animals' lives. But the phenomenon of projecting distinctively human qualities surely does exist. Oddly, it is often animal exploiters who are the most weirdly anthropomorphic, as when a fast food chain uses a rooster singing opera ("Carmen," I believe it is) to advertise chicken sandwiches, or an articulate tuna pleads to be caught, canned, and eaten, or a barbecue establishment displays smiling pictures of a chicken, cow, and pig beneath its name. (The only sense I can make of this grotesque nonsense is that the consumption of happy humanoids can be made sufficiently comic and unreal as to disguise the reality of violent deaths on one's plate.) Companions of animals are also sometimes guilty along with authors of stories for children, but advertising probably is most blatant. The practice ranges from harmless to offensive. Ironically, anti-anthropomorphism displays its own pathetic fallacy: it fails to perceive in animals much that is truly there. In Ruskin's words, it substitutes false appearances for "ordinary, proper, and true appearances."

I asked explicitly above (and implicitly throughout) who we look at when we look at an animal, what do we look for, how can we know what is there? The truly anthropomorphic or pathetically fallacious sees himself or some other erroneous projection. The human failure to apprehend the animalself disrespects him: projecting into his reality treats the animal as an emptiness waiting to be filled; subtracting from his reality treats him as lacking autonomous identity of his own. When, say, John Muir tells of Tamarack Creek running "glad,...rejoicing, exulting, chanting, dancing in white," I recognize metaphor, or what Ruskin called "willful fancy." I can picture him and the water and know what he described and that he deeply admired it. But what about the woodchuck he says "plays and loves," or the rattlesnake he found in his cabin displaying "downright bashfulness and embarrassment"? Anthropomorphism? This is a concept in need of refinement.

A tuna made verbal has suffered the imposition of human qualities—only humans speak this kind of language (and only humans would be likely to act so self-destructively!). Likewise, only humans sing opera, but other animals grace the world with songs of a different sort, so singing is no human monopoly. I think of states such as bashfulness and embarrassment, and wonder how we could claim sole ownership and that finding them in other species represents the attribution of *human* qualities to nonhumans? A snake abashed to be found out of place and vulnerable is a snake abashed—snakely so, not humanly. Neither Muir nor many others who have found animals in such straits will doubt this. Awareness and emotion are waters of existence which creatures variously drink, variously experience, and variously express, each in his own distinctive ways. With Joseph Wood Krutch, who heard the voice and fell under the mystique of desert, we can ask, "Are we so separate from nature that our states are actually discontinuous with it? Is there nothing outside ourselves which is somehow glad or sad? Is it really a fallacy when we attribute to nature feelings analogous to our own?...When he [Wordsworth] was most himself it seemed to him that, on the contrary, the joy of nature was older than the joy of man and that what was transitory in the individual was permanent somewhere else." That must be true. But since it most likely will not be discerned through experimental procedures, because it describes conditions mostly beyond science's reach, how is the truth apprehended?

DISPOSABLE ANIMALS

Wendell Berry has spoken of the importance of affection in a person's relation with the land, if he would know it and have it remain productive, healthy, and beautiful. And Ruskin knew that, "The more we can feel, the more beauty we shall perceive in this universal frame. No man knows how lovely Nature is who has not entwined her with his heart." If we are to give animals their due it will be because we look at them as they are in their own right, allow our-selves the natural feelings of appreciation and civility for fellow sojourners, and see that humans share and do not own reality. We can pacify the "violent feelings" that Ruskin described as precursors to false perceptions of nature by being attentive and willing to be moved by what we see.

Right relation with the other animals cannot depend on their measure of humanness, but rather on a recovery of the old vision and veritable experience of a shared life and spirit, participated in by all, and by respect for their unique revelation of it. As Berry poetically said in "Healing," health and holiness "can only be held in common," and the human's job "is to respect oneself as a creature, no more and no less."

Respect *all* creatures. *All* creation.

REFERENCES

Berry, Wendell. *What Are People For?* San Francisco: North Point Press, 1990.

Cook, E.T. & A. Wedderburn. (eds.). *The Works of John Ruskin.* London: George Allen, 1904. Vols. I & V.

Kennedy, J.S. *The New Anthropomorphism.* Cambridge: Cambridge University Press, 1992.

Krutch, Joseph Wood. *The Voice of the Desert.* New York: Morrow Quill Paperbacks, 1955.

Mighetto, Lisa (ed.). *Muir Among the Animals.* San Francisco: Sierra Club Books, 1986.

Muir, John. *My First Summer in the Sierra.* New York: Penguin Books, 1987.

Thomas, Keith. *Man and the Natural World: A History of the Modern Sensibility.* New York: Pantheon Books, 1983.

Thoreau, Henry David. *Walden and Civil Disobedience.* New York: Airmont Publishing Co., 1965.

10

CREATURES OF BIG HART CANYON

The canyon emerges, descends gradually, and then plunges, all virtually within shouting range of its inception. I will be camped here two days before I venture in, anticipating my entrance while first renewing my appreciation of other parts of this favored place. I have been away too long.

A quarter-mile square, forty acres of southern Sierra Nevada wilderness in the Piute Mountains, the land is remote and nearly undisturbed. It lies a tortuous hour's drive—ten miles—from the nearest full-time neighbor at the end of a meager, single-lane pathway that has long forgotten its last encounter with a blade. Only minor signs of predecessors remain.

I first saw it in spring, vibrant with wildflowers and quivering agave seed stalks. The land is richly textured with granite that has been colorfully splashed with lichen and pinked from its primal subterranean brewing. Thick with juniper and mixed species of pine and oak, it rests at 5,500 feet with a ridge north at 7,000 and a valley below at 3,500. A transition zone, diverse and dry.

My affection was first aroused by Big Hart Canyon, bisector and definitive feature of this ground. Born below a spring in the meadow just to the north, it begins as a modestly swelling stream-cut. Then it grows bolder with a granite monolith guiding the water around itself and into the shadows beyond—a dramatic touch reminiscent of ranches that announce themselves with muscular gateways, but natural in this setting. Live oak and rill descend through a jumble of rock, cascades, fallen trees, tall grasses, and flowers. I clambered its length twice that first day, then spiraled around it up to a point where I could see the whole canyon embedded, enfolded as a crease within a wandering landscape. In semiarid country the little waterway inside its narrow and deepening crevasse stands out; it makes a distinctive biome, a creative expression of granite and gravity, geological patience coupled with biological exuberance. It entranced me.

Today I enter from the meadow and am soon halted abruptly just below the first waterfall. Certain sounds vibrate with authority and in this country a sibilant rattle rivets your attention. I have been moving down the canyon slowly in order fully to appreciate it and out of concern for the uncertain footing. Annie, fifty pounds of canine enthusiasm, moves ahead and less prudently. As she bounds over a ledge I hear simultaneously the thump of her landing and a vigorous maraca greeting. She has dropped virtually into a snake's coiled midst. Momentum carried her beyond, curiosity drew her back, "ANNIE COME!" impelled her to me. We eased into an upward arc where we could safely look down upon an angry, thickset, and probably mortified rattlesnake. He buzzed resoundingly and fearsomely, but the great jaws were fully occupied with the hindmost end of a half-ingested rodent. He seemed vulnerable, and I wondered if discreet silence might have been better advised. (Or is rattling just what one does at these moments, caution be damned?) The threatening rasp went on; he stared fear and warning but neither spat nor swallowed: a snake's version of caught with his pants down.

I walk on even more slowly now. There are fewer flowers this dry year but tree shade, rock shadow, and a secure feeling of earthy enclosure remain. A little farther and Big Hart's heart, the old canyon's dramatic center, unfolds. Shape of V opens to U. I work my way down to a smoothed rock surface about thirty yards long and half that wide, trees on the east slope, bouldered wall on the west, a vast falling vista to the south over rock parapet. Abyss ahead and to the right, while a slick granite slide descends steeply for two hundred feet on the left. The stream that found and helped shape a crease across the rock floor does it here, too, snake-like down the slide. Near bottom it drops into a shallow basin, rolls over and down a short expanse, pools again, pauses, disappears south. Big Hart Canyon graces other land below mine, but differently: a more restrained drop and less green shade but still impressive. I slip through the west side rock and cautiously make my way down to the slide's base.

When land changes shape and cover as this does there are always new ways to wander. After some time gazing up and around from the pool I head west again. Using both hands and feet I ascend the steep canyon side, find a cow trail, and return to camp through the meadow.

This meadow has particular appeal, something like an indeterminate promise. An expanse of thirty or so acres, encircled by oak and pine, with a few great ponderosas scattered about, it is veined by the main spring flow and one or two occasional subsidiaries. It reaches southeast to just north of my place. I learned something there the first morning we camped here over a year ago: live oak with a black bear cub scuttling up it in fear and mother bear launched from under it in protective fury is never again just a tree. It amplifies to oak-bear site, a place to pause quietly on approach. I have come to it most respectfully ever since that dawn encounter.

Up early that first morning, Ann and I grabbed coffee and meandered, led by Annie and second dog Mara. As we approached what was still only a tree, a sprawling old live oak with branches arching to the ground, the dogs dashed under thinking they had found a chaseable creature. Thus, cub ascending. Predictably, his mother took offense. My recognition of the tree's transformation began with Annie and Mara's frantic emergence from beneath it beelining for me with mother in chase. She stopped, and turned back toward the cub. Annie, rarely aggressive but always ebullient, halted and headed back after her, whether in play or misguided predation I will never know. Mara, a Lab crippled by hip dysplasia only partially corrected by surgery, normally moves like a slow breeze through dense forest, but unlike Annie she fully understood the mistake they had made and did not hesitate in her labored course back, her movements more lively than usual, I thought. Mother turned to pursue Annie, who finally realized she had misread the situation and shot past me in the direction of a retreating Ann.

Still rooted paralytically where I was when this began, I see Mara five yards in front of me, mother bear five yards behind her, every creature around except the cub and me in frenzied motion. As Mara heaved by, the bear halted, we looked inquiringly at each other, she turned back to her cub. Regaining breath and mobility, I turned and fell flat over a sagebrush. In a few minutes we heard mother calling youngster down from the tree. When we come camping now the dogs always lie facing north toward that spot, lest she be there and remember.

Oak-bear place. On another visit, staked out with camera, we saw a lone bear cross the meadow toward the spring. Today when I pass through a brawny hawk calls and flies up to watch me from the top of a pine. This meadow has a mysterious feel to it, and the spirit and power of these animals compose that in great part. For millennia people have believed, and I am among them, that countless species have existed through numberless years, and still do now in plenitude and beauty, because life's creative spirit requires this kind of abundance to express itself adequately. Creation is *one*, speaking with diverse voices. Without bear and hawk the meadow would be subdued, diminished. Yet by choice industrial-era humans do daily violence to beings by the millions, with needless killing and perhaps precipitating a sixth great extinction. A depth of suffering and loss hard to fathom, bought by our errant notions of the good for humans.

This visit is my first in several months. I tried to get up here twice during the winter but found it snowed in. Then I moved 1,200 miles north. As I drove south and realized experientially the distance between new home and land I thought of selling it: too expensive, too infrequent, too far. But I will not: too resonant, too much Hart and soul to relinquish. I knew it within an hour of arrival three days ago. It galvanized my senses and drew waves of emotion from my gut that turned into gratitude's tears.

Except for Annie I came alone and ironically have not seen so many couples since leading marriage preparation workshops years ago. First evening, out of the valley to the east, a pair of red-tailed hawks ascend riding the air and float circuitously. Then one plunges toward the other, startling me—mock aggression, it seemed, part of their airy ritual. They appear to touch gently and then separate and soar synchronously. They fly these artful motions for several minutes, as if dancing, then one wings north while the other keeps circling. Astonished, I mull in wonder.

Within moments a *whirr-r-r-r*—a pair of California Quail breeze through and alight on the path a few yards away. He assumes a watchful pose on a rock, she eats obliviously. Eventually he joins her at the meal but remains vigilant throughout: peck, peck, look around, peck. Each evening around 6:00 they make this same entrance, follow these same protocols. She is plump. He is sleek and protective.

I watch a pair of western tanagers as they flit about and watch me from the pines. Gaudy in their black, red, and yellow, but so timid I would think subdued colors better suited their personalities. Who knows what value their flamboyance has for them? Last evening I was fortunate to look up from my book just as they quietly barreled over. Playing and courting, twice joining, parting: another dance. Affection exchanged, perhaps love.

To my delight the show continues. A pair of western bluebirds arrive, take turns hovering curiously above me, then depart. Finches and warblers, scrub jays and rufous-sided towhees, unidentifieds. I feel as though camped within an avian love song. Their devotion inspires me. At home I have seen cardinal couples up to their knees in a feeder, when gently the male offers seed from his beak to hers. Why does he do that? Why hawks and tanagers dancing? Why ask? Are they so utterly different from us? Jaw-dropping awe at the pleasing, perplexing rightness of such natural things just gives them their due.

Annie ends my reverie with a burst of foul breath as she returns from her rounds. The day before yesterday, that began with the bang of rattlesnake encounter, ended with a whimper still odorously echoed. I was watching birds at dusk and looked up the path to see Annie in her stalking pose. Typically this precedes a futile assault upon squirrels. She leaned over the path's edge glaring, still as sculpture. I could not see her intended prey. She launched, but atypically boomeranged immediately, foaming at the mouth and wanting my assistance. She plowed the ground with her snout, dug frantically for looser dirt, circled, plowed, tunneled through a pile of pine straw, then dug some more. She had absorbed a direct hit to the mouth. A silent skunk has resounding effects on a dog's composure and breath.

Twice during the night she arose to vomit. Now she is fine, except for her breath. I wonder if a rodent grapevine spreads the news of justice rendered, and if it also speaks of the snake and his victim?

The mountain north has a spot I like for its view and setting and this time of year its wildflowers. As morning clouds lift from its shoulders I fill my pack with water and food, paper and pencil, and cross through the meadow. The hawk calls warning as once again she lifts to the top of a ponderosa, and I stand admiring through binoculars and trying to locate the nest I suppose she protects. I cannot find it and have disturbed her enough; I head northwest up the steep mountainside.

Climbing to the ridge I follow a trail up through meadows separated by bands of granite outcropping interspersed with trees and eventually arrive almost due north of camp, 1,200 feet higher and perhaps a mile away on line of sight. A tremendous view south into the Tehachapi Mountains with their persistent haze. Much of that is natural but I always suspect drifting infusion of Central Valley pollution, a serious and shameful matter. A steeply falling little glade lies directly before me decorated by lupine and assorted consorts. I write in the shade of a live oak perfectly disposed for my purposes. Ground squirrels and birds *chirr*, sun shines, breeze woos leaf and needle.

Four days here without sight of another human, yet I have the distinct sense of companionship. Occasionally eerie, it leads to reflection, alertness, a sense of appreciative connectedness. I can no more imagine flourishing without this contact than without other humans. Rooted in dirt and mystery, this natural world speaks of most that we need to hear. Why not respond to such voices?

I return by the meadow and notice signs cows have been through. Since I quit eating them, I can think of but one quasi-positive thing about these animals. Occasionally, when I bushwhack through dense brush or over unstable footing, I intersect one of their trails and the going gets easier. But I would trade that in an instant for their disappearance from here. They shit prodigiously, trample down the earth, foul the spring, crush wildflowers, and chomp off the agave's seed stalk—unforgivable since each plant has but one progenitive opportunity then dies, in this case, like a salmon before spawning. What a strange law that makes it my responsibility rather than the cattleman's to keep them away.

Withal, they deserve pity and liberation from their fate. Part nature and part artifact, lives nasty, brutish, and short, and climaxed in slaughter. (Here on this mountain maybe not so nasty and brutish but still short and with the same terminus.) Like all domesticated animals they are diminished versions of their ancient progenitors. We treat them shamelessly, as if mere objects, and show a decent respect neither for them nor the land and indigenous creatures hurt by their presence.

Days pass, time shortens; I must leave. This last morning I rise to a heavy dew, so wet it could almost have showered. Fog drifts in and rolls out. I start a fire to warm and illuminate as only campfires can. Later I walk down into the side of the canyon.

Though I usually feel well acquainted with this land and all its aspects, random walks reveal new perspectives and visions. This time I find a mystic garden spot below the first waterfall, above the snake's ledge but on the east side. I hear without seeing the water and look across through trees toward gleaming efflorescence. Even Annie stills, as if moved in uncommon ways for her, but time will not slow. We walk. An acorn woodpecker, the first I have seen, alights on a pine snag and searches. On into the meadow, hawk silent, maybe aware she has outlasted me.

I pack and leave slowly, taking an hour and a half to drive the eighteen miles down and out of this range into the desert. I think of the meadow and its oak-bear grove, recollect my "bearanoid" hikes in Alaska. What is a right relation between humans and nonhumans? What do we gain and lose living predominantly in a constructed world, designed and subdued for ourselves? I am convinced by the meadow and canyon that they can help me fathom the inherent meanings and values, the world's mysterious otherness, autonomy, and occasional fearsomeness, existing in its own excellent ways. Sharing Earth we should identify with the others.

The animals' presence wove this visit whole. I wanted solitude, and except for airplanes and noise of dirt bike one day in the distance, I have had no awareness of other people for a week. And I never felt alone. I fear the snake's venom and the bear's strength, but both land and experience would be impoverished without their powerful presence. Hawk, skunk, even Annie: each is part of the fullness.

A few days before I left for here, as I arrived at work, I was drawn to a pond where violet green swallows swept the air for breakfast. I had not known them before. First evening on the mountain I sip wine and recover from the miles, then realize I am haloed by violet green flight. It seemed a greeting and a linking, another revelation of Earth wonder.

PART THREE

DISPOSABILITY'S CONTEXT

11

THE WESTERN WAY WITH THE WORLD

[Note: The next three chapters contain what will be familiar themes because I wrote them before finishing Part One. The account in Part Three provides the detail from which chapters three and four were drawn. While my chief concern was to advocate a new way for animal welfare to intervene for companion animals, I was also drawn to understand more about the cultural context which inspired "euthanasia" and other kinds of culturally accepted practices that seem similarly destructive and self- and species-centered. The theme for the present chapter developed as I thought about two characteristics of killing as an acceptable solution to problems of surplus animals: first, it represents a dramatic form of dominance in the relation of humans to other creatures, and second, as it is performed by animal welfarists the killing appears to be a form of cooptation on behalf of societal desires to have and dispose of "pets" in a manner not unlike Western culture's traditional relations with "otherness" and nature in general.

The incursion of Europeans in the late fifteenth century into the Western Hemisphere exemplified aggressive domination fueled by ambition and ethnocentrism. In studying this era I began to see the missionary's role relative to natives in the Spanish arm of the invasion as somewhat parallel to the animal protectors' role relative to animals in the humane society. Each conceived himself as serving a high and compassionate purpose on behalf of vulnerable creatures. Yet on the whole the effects were contrary to those creatures' primary interests while the rescuers' societies' interests were served rather well. Both looked like versions of cooptation.

I am less satisfied with this parallel now than I was originally, but I remain strongly persuaded that the European invasion was a dramatic expression of the controlling dynamic and world view of Western culture whenever aspiration meets either wanted object or impediment. Simply put, "If you want it, take it; if something's in the way, shove it aside." Justifications range from science to religion, from race to species to progress, and all are deadly. Companion animals are but one of the victims.]

~

A tragic and still unfinished history of deadly dominance under the guise of a greater good erupted onto what would become the Americas half a millennium ago. This history of interhuman relations may reveal in greater relief than its interspecies counterpart the progression and justification of extreme and bizarre behaviors. Many who participated in the making of that history, missionaries in particular, believed they acted with only the best interests of its victims in mind, in accord with God's will.

European imperialism in the Western Hemisphere marched under a civilizing banner baroquely woven by Christian institutions, functionaries, and ideology in league with state sponsors. "God, Glory, and Gold" was the declared tripartite motivation for Spanish conquest; God provided essential mystification and justification for the enterprise. The solitary God of Christianity, said the Catholic emissaries, yearned only for salvation of native souls. But converting those unaware of the need while simultaneously serving many masters was a complicated business.

From the initial encounters in the Caribbean forward, terrible things happened to native populations in the wake of Spanish rapacity and disease. To their credit, I suppose, despite the eventual indigenous calamity, Spanish theologians and philosophers looked west and surveyed a mystery. According to historian Lewis Hanke, they wondered about the natives: "Who were they? Whence came they? What was their nature, their capacity for Christianity and European civilization? Most important of all, what relationship would be the right one for the Spaniards to establish with them?" Whatever the answer, the forward movement did not hesitate. Respectful withdrawal, even a thoughtful pause, was unimaginable. After all, Pope Alexander VI, barely a year after Columbus' first contact, "by the authority of Almighty God" had granted the Spanish monarchy all the lands found and waiting to be found along with responsibility for native souls. This was breathtaking audacity but not unique—Columbus had already claimed everything and everyone in sight and planted the Spanish and Catholic ensigns on the beach in the presence of the islands' perplexed, and now expropriated, residents.

Bartoleme de Las Casas, Dominican friar, spent close to fifty years in New Spain early in the conquest (until 1547) and was by far the most emphatic and articulate defender of native rights to liberty and property. He wrote prolifically, formally debated and informally argued for their humanity, and interceded on their behalf with kings and popes. Even so, until late in his long life he did not question the legitimacy of the Spanish intrusion into the New World. He believed in papal authority over all humans on Earth and in Christianity as the one true religion. He was convinced that the natives required conversion for the sake of their eternal souls and would in time peacefully embrace subjection to Crown and Cross, and that though essentially barbarian the natives were like "uncultivated soil" that with gentle effort could yield Christian fruit. Las Casas was their greatest advocate, but the fact that such foundational beliefs tended to violate the "infidels" apparently escaped him. Though opposed by Las Casas, a "just war" against recalcitrant natives was launched in order to expedite their salvation.

What sort of beings were the natives? Cotton Mather, farther north and years later, described them as "ravenous howling wolves." Sepulveda, prominent Spanish aristocrat and scholar, in debate with Las Casas at Valladolid in 1550, argued that they were natural slaves in the Aristotelian sense.

They were inherently rude, inferior, and barbarous, and suited only to serve their natural superiors. Some argued they were human only in form—more like beasts, or children, or women than true men. Father Juan Nentuig, who worked many years with natives of Sonora in northwestern Mexico in the late eighteenth century, was superficially knowledgeable and sympathetic toward them. Yet he considered them simple, superstitious, and silly in their beliefs. Their character pivoted around four foundations, he declared: "ignorance, ingratitude, inconstancy, and laziness."

In short, the Europeans had little doubt that they faced creatures who were radically different from and inferior to themselves. Such a fatefully dangerous premise led in time to an overall population collapse of around 95%—tens of millions of people lost within less than a century of contact.

Spaniards construed the violence as a just war for native conversion. Despite their ravenous pursuit of "gold and glory," they viewed their intrusion as a civilizing and Christianizing enterprise for the sake of the natives. For many this served only as a rhetorical veneer for ambition and duplicity.

Luis Rivera describes how the Spaniards redefined native political rebellion as religious apostasy; this was their "escape hatch" when war and native enslavement became necessary to restrain their ungrateful and heathen impulses. Similarly, in 1573 the "conquest" was by ordinance relabeled "pacification" (echoed 400 years later in word and deed in Viet Nam). More than simple hypocrisy occurs in this. The Spaniards were intensely legalistic and Catholic and needed to portray themselves as just and beneficent. Where the ancients saw the world divided between civilized and barbarian, the European, particularly Spanish, dualistic hierarchy was Christian and non-Christian. This distinction by itself tended to justify aggressive action against (on behalf of) infidels. However, more was required to address the question of method: how to *justly* execute soul-saving aggression.

Into the breach in 1513 came *El Requerimiento*, the official procedure for properly converting native infidels. More an emollient for jurist and theologian discomfort back home in Spain than a mellowing influence on the ground far west, it was meant seriously. As an expression of the self-deception and risks involved in paternalistic doing-for-the-sake-of-others (even when it kills them), it fascinates.

El Requerimiento (The Requirement) was intended as the official statement made to natives upon initial contact with Spaniards. That these non-Spanish-speakers could not possibly comprehend what their visitors required of them was apparently immaterial to legalism's artful logic. The statement began with an explanation of how the one true God created the world and placed it and all people and everything under authority of the Pope in Rome, who, by the way, had recently granted the natives and their land to the Spanish monarch. It continued:

> I beg and require of you...to recognize the church as lady and superior of the universe and to acknowledge the Supreme Pontiff, called pope, in her name, and the king and queen...as lords and superiors...and consent to have these religious fathers declare and preach these things to you. If you do so you will be acting well, and those who are over you and to whom you owe obedience...would welcome you with love and charity. If you do not do it...then with the help of God I will undertake powerful action against you. I will make war on you everywhere and in every way that I can. I will subject you to the yoke and obedience of the church and of Their Highnesses. I will take you personally and your wives and children, and make slaves of you, and as such sell you off...and I will take away your property and cause you all the evil and harm I can.

A hard offer to refuse; straightforward and unambiguous if you understood the Spanish language and mentality. It bespoke a strange messianism. And under its grace atrocities occurred that on occasion led evangelized natives to declare that if heaven was where Christians went upon dying, they preferred hell.

From Columbus and Cortez to Las Casas and beyond, a sense of providential empowerment infused action. A divine plan had seemingly arranged contact with these new lands and peoples. With native salvation as the end, hardly any means was proscribed. Pope Clement VII in 1529 recognized that in order to bring barbarians to God missionaries and soldiers could act "through force and arms if necessary so that their souls may share in the kingdom of heaven." In early seventeenth-century Chile, "The very same rebellious Indians [the Araucans] given as slaves would enjoy great spiritual well-being because they would be instructed and taught the things of our faith," said Felipe III. Jose de Acosta, a late sixteenth- century missionary stated: "It is necessary to use the whip....In this way they are forced to enter salvation even if it is against their will." Defending the *encomienda* (a grant of land and natives but not technically slavery), a Dominican theologian noticed that without Spanish domination the natives soon lost their Catholic faith, but without forced labor to work the land and mines there would be no Spaniards around to maintain the dominion. Thus, no forced labor, no Spaniards, no native salvation.

Even without salvation as a factor, there are still many who consider it reasonable to kill for God. ("Salvation" today, as often as not, is exported and imposed by disciples of economic development, usually with results similar to those of earlier evangelists.) But most who take spirituality humbly as well as seriously will find it incongruous to link its nurture with aggression. Similarly, one assumes a large, problematic burden when he chooses to act beneficently on behalf of another in matters of life and death, whether a missionary thinking to redeem unrecognized spiritual need within benighted natives or an animal welfarist prepared to kill a healthy animal to protect her from potential suffering. The road to error is sometimes paved with good intention.

As the bearers of "cross and sword" settled into the new lands, ecclesiastics from Franciscan, Dominican, Augustinian, and Jesuit orders continued to proselytize and form mission communities (analogous in many ways to animal shelters) which natives were either encouraged or required to join. Assuming a variety of forms depending on location, native propensities, natural resources, and missionary inclinations, missions had in common a requirement of obedience to the priest. The presence of soldiers facilitated native compliance.

Referred to as "reductions" or "congregations" by the Spaniards, missions were totalistic organizations. They endeavored to utterly transform native ways. We do not fully appreciate the weight of their intended effects without realizing that in European eyes the indigenous peoples had no substantial political, religious, economic, or civic order that it was their task to replace. Rather, they labored to fill a vacuum, to impart value, order, religion, morals, and purpose to folk either empty, misled, or simply childlike. The natives were seen as beings hardly conceivable as subjects of lives. Where the natives lived, in what kinds of structures, what they wore and ate, how they celebrated and mourned, the locus of their sacrality, attitudes toward work, property, and trade—the missionaries had all these responsibilities to fulfill, although not requested by the recipients.

One area of mission caretaking often welcomed by natives concerned caretaker-induced calamities. Epidemic diseases imported by their benefactors, chiefly smallpox, measles, typhus, and influenza, periodically swept native communities. Sickness and malnutrition combined with demoralization from shattered ways of life and left people truly in need of succor, spiritual and material. Priests offered it, often effectively. To a degree they also offered protection against exploitative Spaniards in the vicinity. Still, under the circumstances, only righting somewhat one's wrongs was small recompense.

Missions in coordination with governmental offices intended to relocate, educate, Christianize, and control native peoples. Not incidentally, they served economic purposes as well. A labor source for mines, fields, and households, in some missions men were required to work three days supporting themselves and three for the interlopers. Their "laziness" continually exasperated the Spaniards, who did not believe in hard labors for themselves but who did enjoy accumulating surpluses for trade, taxes, and personal gain off the sweat of others.

Unfortunately for all concerned, particularly the natives, the mortality rate among mission inhabitants was such that indoctrination in the faith, let alone economic productivity, was hard to accomplish. The historians Paul Farnsworth and Robert Jackson described missions in Alta California as "resettlement...into what in effect were death camps." And as they and many others note, when economic goals conflicted with cultural and spiritual ones, the latter were generally postponed. Always paramount was "turning them into a docile, Christian, peasant labor force. The missions failed in the goal of cultural change but did succeed in using native labor to finance the colonization of the region." Akin to being required to buy the rope with which you will be hanged.

While Euro-American and Spanish cultures were very different, both were Christian and both inflicted domination on others, who they would not see as rights-holding humans, through consolidation and negation. Yet Iberians, particularly the missionaries, believed they were doing good for the native other. Whatever happened to their bodies, at least their souls were saved from eternal damnation and suffering. Luis Rivera recounts some of the strange extremes reached in these imposed salvational frenzies. Caupolican, sixteenth-century Araucan chief, fought and lost, was captured and finally converted, causing "great joy among the Spaniards, who after instructing him in his new religion, baptizing him, and celebrating his conversion, proceeded nevertheless to execute him in a horrendous way: by impalement and transfixment with arrows." Similarly, Cuauhtemoc the Aztec monarch and Atahualpa the Inka king were baptized before execution, in the latter instance "by hanging and burning. [Then] he is buried as a Christian, with the appropriate liturgical ceremonies."

In Riveras' view, the Spaniards spiritualized the sword and politicized the cross. Goodpasture called it the "medieval synthesis," the Crown evangelizing, the church governing. "With the help of the missionary friars, the conquerors pacified and evangelized the Indians, and also extracted their labor." To an extent this merely tells a story of corruption and evil, the laying on of a patina of godly justification for caesarly aspiration. But can we doubt that many a friar devoutly believed, and that his devotion unwittingly served very different purposes? More than served—enabled and legitimized them?

In contrast to the mission system as a means to control natives, the eventual Anglo-American format for colonization and confiscation became the reservation. The effect of the first generations of European immigrants on native populations farther north was much the same as the Spaniards' had been—on average only around 5% of the precontact millions survived. But the attitude toward these indigenous people was quite different.

Spaniards saw souls to save—however hypocritical or thin this concern, it was not empty—and backs to be bent for extraction of mineral and other wealth. Native decimation was largely inadvertent—they were so plentiful and evoked so little respect. But they had economic value and their salvation, if not their lives, pleased the Christian God.

British and Americans, on the other hand, civilized and Christianized as an afterthought, when at all. David Stannard says that for the British the natives were "at best, a superfluous population." Like a stump in a field or a stone in a furrow, the natives were in their way. Where some medieval Christians had believed animals were given life only as God's way to keep the meat fresh until they ate them, these moderns saw native sickness and dying as God's cleansing act preparatory to His willed occupation of the land by the chosen. (Conveniently, others' living *and* dying served Christian needs.) They never thought to incorporate the inhabitants of the newly found lands into the new order. Rather, native peoples were fated for death or exportation to the far-seeming lands west of the Mississippi: the "Indian Territory." This isolation policy finally evolved into the reservation, forced quarantine on the least desirable land, and natives became wards of the Indian Bureau. It was a vast continent, but not as big as the intruders' compulsion to possess.

According to most accounts, initial European reactions to natives tended to be positive. They were seen as rather enviable innocents living edenic existences. Since the natives typically received them hospitably and often provided vital instruction on surviving in the new-for-them world, their virtues were hard to deny. But, of course, this passed quickly.

An interesting contrast in perception commonly characterized these encounters. The native asked if he confronted *men* or *gods* (and learned soon enough from experience the radical this-worldliness of the intruders). Emblematic of the Western world view, the European asked instead whether the other was *man* or *beast.*

According to Hanke "the idea of the unfitness of natives and their inferiority to Europeans appeared in whatever far corners of the world Europeans reached." In *Machines as the Measure of Men* historian Michael Adas confirms Hanke as he surveys the role of scientific and technological superiority as the justification for imperialism in Africa, India, and China. Finally, Rivera cites Beatriz Pastor in her study of the conquest: "It would become the metamorphosis of man into a thing, passing through a first metamorphosis of man into a beast...which would climax in the transformation of man into a commodity." Rivera understands these ways of thinking as "ideological mechanism[s] of domination."

Domination and using continue to characterize Western ways of thinking and acting toward others. Implicitly this requires considering oneself separate and superior to others. Combine this with a lost sense of sacredness or intrinsic value, and exploitation and aggression will easily follow. Conflicting ideas are found side by side in this. The modern world places commodity values at its center but refuses to abandon a semblance of ideals. Companion animals fall into this contradiction and are disposed of: carelessly by egocentric guardians, caringly by animal welfarists "for their own good."

More than once as I looked at the history of European and American incursions on the people and land of this hemisphere, the specter of the Viet Nam War arose in parallel. Who can forget the televised military man explaining the day's action: "We had to destroy the village in order to save it"? The good served in its saving—the good of most Western assaults on nature and peoples and value—is far from clear, especially as we view the costs.

REFERENCES

Adas, Michael. *Machines as the Measure of Men.* Ithica: Cornell University Press, 1989.

Goodpasture, H. McKennie. *Cross and Sword.* Maryknoll, NY: Orbis Books, 1989.

Hanke, Lewis. *Aristotle and the American Indians: A Study in Race Prejudice.* Bloomington: Indiana University Press, 1959.

Hefner, Robert (ed.). *Conversion to Christianity.* Berkeley: University of California Press, 1993.

Hu-Dehart, Evelyn. *Missionaries, Miners, and Indians.* Tucson: University of Arizona Press, 1981.

Langer, E. & R. Jackson (ed.). *The New Latin American Mission History.* Lincoln: University of Nebraska Press, 1995.

Rivera, Luis. *A Violent Evangelism: The Political and Religious Conquest of the Americas.* Louisville: Westminster/John Knox Press, 1992. Citation from: Beatriz Pastor. *Discurso Narrativo de la Conquista de America.* La Habana: Casa de las Americas, 1984.

Spicer, Edward. *Cycles of Conquest.* Tucson: University of Arizona Press, 1962.

Stannard, David. *American Holocaust.* New York: Oxford University Press, 1992.

Traboulay, David M. *Columbus and Las Casas.* Lanham, MD: University Press of America, 1994.

12

DETACHMENT AND THE
MERCHANDISING OF MEANING

To respectfully paraphrase an ancient Hebrew query: Was man made for the economy? Or was the economy made for man? (It was the Sabbath they asked about.) In a similar vein I borrow from one of the scientists on the Manhattan Project: The economy (he spoke of technology) makes a wonderful servant but a terrible master.

Which is servant, which is master? We have already heard the answer from Port Gamble, Washington and Comfort, Texas. Another illustration of inverted values appeared on a large billboard recently. In the background was an outline of a house but neither that nor the name of the sponsoring business, presumably a bank or mortgage company, caught your attention. In the foreground a woman, oddly 1950s style, strode forcefully out at the viewer with a briefcase in hand and a look on her face of triumph/ecstasy/power, maybe even transcendence. To her right in large cursive letters were these reassuring words: "I CAN AFFORD IT!" A potent piece of advertising and all the more annoying for its probable effectiveness. It promises artificial achievements: mastery and fulfillment through a monetary medium. While the market will probably drive Port Gamble away from all that has given it value over a century and a half, but toward maximum corporate profitability, here we are to believe the market will carry this dazzled woman to completeness.

Similar examples of overgrown and cannibalizing commerce assault us unendingly. We are hardly conscious of them anymore. But cultural phenomena connect in sometimes surprising ways, and it is worth looking at certain associations between our servant relationship to money values and our impoverishment of others.

I cited John Rodman's observation earlier "that the same basic principles are manifested in quite diverse forms." That came to mind as I reached the end of a trail through shaded twilight of ancient forest one day and stepped into light that should not have been there. I had reached the boundary of Olympic National Park, and beyond that border every tree was gone, felled and carted off to market. In that moment of grief and rage I knew viscerally that Rodman was right. I saw mob violence and street crime and recognized the continuity with these clear-cut ravages.

Those "same basic principles" represent patterns of dividedness and hierarchy, a vision of the world as merely a collection of resources to be gathered and transformed for use and profit. Consumer culture, founded on these principles and immersed in "commodity fetishism," moves relationships inexorably toward commodification. As relations are increasingly experienced in this fashion, they are used and discarded as commodities. In Elizabeth Anderson's words, commodity fetishism "consists in a blind devotion to consumer goods, attributing powers and values to them that are properly to be found in relations among people." I think these values are not restricted to relations among people; they are found wherever respect defines relations (as toward nature and animals).

The preoccupation with commodities and with using cuts a wide swath. It shoulders aside other values and takes over. It has powerful sponsors in the form of fetishism's most ardent devotees, those who not only are beguiled by commodities themselves but who profit when others are persuaded to use as well. This is why so much of the recent lamentation by some about the decline of character and virtue (in others) and the desperate need for their resurrection sounds hollow. They are correct to affirm the values, but so long as they fail to ask what we lost them to, the exhortation can have little effect. Like an alcoholic worried about his health who wants to discuss exercise and diet and curative time in the sun, but who denies his addiction and its effects, the apostles of virtue will gain little without cultural "sobriety."

Fetishism and the detachment it brings are a large part of the syndrome underlying so much that is destructive in our time, including mass killing of our animal companions and the host of social pathologies that afflict us. There does not appear to be a single aspiration, however elevated, for which a commodity surrogate will not be offered and too often accepted. How does this come to be?

By most accounts the commodification of American culture achieved ballistic momentum following World War II. It did not begin then certainly; strains of individualistic acquisitiveness were apparent from near the beginning. But after the stringencies of depression and war, a burst of need satisfaction and self-indulgence seems predictable. The development of that burst into a state of permanent and frantic consumerism, however, is more difficult to understand. And if frantic seems too strong a word, listen for the sound of tremulous anxiety in the voices of business reporters any time quarterly economic indicators pause for a figurative breath. Non-growth appears to threaten collapse into an abyss of non-meaning.

Historians such as Christopher Lasch in his study of the progress mystique, *The True and Only Heaven*, show that the science-technology-commodity bandwagon had dissenters for hundreds of years, and that they lost the debate. And Max Weber's work early in the twentieth century on the relation between Protestantism and economic life offers a distinctive view of our willingness to consecrate the market realm. He says that capitalism, particularly its American version, creates reversals in the natural order of things. Acquisition of money, objects, and services, rather than serving as the means to satisfy needs, becomes an end in itself. Work tends to lose its expressive and instrumental functions and becomes a self-justifying and absorbing duty. So both production and consumption are cut loose from their original functions and take on lives of their own, with neither intended to facilitate "spontaneous enjoyment of life." To make things worse, until the mid-nineteenth century capitalism had remained rooted in traditional and leisurely practices which were driven out by a new spirit of competitive expansiveness among a few. Others, fearing for their survival in such a milieu, were induced to act in similar fashion. As the new ethos took over it seemed to exemplify an inherent bias that would drive the entire system in new and negative directions, a kind of Gresham's Law phenomenon: bad but competitively effective practices drive out good. The commodity ethos is rich at growth but poor at ethical assessment.

Weber believed he found the roots of the "iron cage" of acquisitive and work-centered existence in Puritan asceticism. Work glorifies God and obeys His assignment of individual callings; dedication to the calling demonstrates one's virtue as success demonstrates His favor. Since His gifts are a form of command, one must take any available opportunity to use them to increase profit and be their worthy steward. This does not include, however, enjoying either the work or its fruits. Material success falls into error when it leads to merriment or idleness; these are sin itself since they reduce the glory one can offer God through labor and also may open the door to other temptations.

Before dismissing this as quaint anachronism, long surpassed by modern economic man, try making the concepts more this-worldly. Omit God and sin, while retaining their secular counterparts. Think of work, joy, and the use of time today. Remember Juliet Schor's findings about "the overworked American" and consider the modern obsession with busyness. You can see how little present experience falls into the category of joy. In constant dollars we are more than twice as affluent on average than we were in 1950 and consume and possess more than twice as much. But I know of no measures of personal satisfactions on balance or of cultural or social indicators that suggest we are doing as well now as then. Apparently we're not very good at materialistic hedonism, despite our enthusiasm.

Work in the Puritan scheme was for the sake of God and soul. Profit, power, and material needs satisfaction were present but secondary. The future prospects of one's soul were best ensured through a concentration on work, not gain, since this both glorified God and strengthened the self-control necessary to ward off worldliness. What is work for us today?

People are often surprised to learn that members of traditional cultures generally worked considerably less than we moderns. Leisure for visiting, ritual, play, story-telling, and celebration mattered more than working and accumulating. According to Weber, "to sink into the grave weighed down with a great material load of money and goods, seems to him [traditional man] explicable only as the product of a perverse instinct." Even until fifty or so years ago, the issue of translating productivity increases into reduced work hours was still alive among labor unions, intellectuals, and others. Today it has currency only as weary fantasy. Schor's figures indicate that during the late 1960s to late 1980s the average employed American increased his or her annual hours by the equivalent of a month: 163 extra hours.

Having more than doubled productivity, we theoretically could work half as much as we did four decades ago for the same quantitative standard of living. Instead we work more. Why? The inherent bias of competition-driven systems toward frantic and unpleasant economic dynamics is one reason.

For example, if I an employer have five people doing my company's work at forty hours per week each, it will give me a competitive advantage, briefly anyway, to lay off one and expect the remaining four to work fifty-hour weeks at the same salaries. I gain forty free hours of work, reduce personnel costs 20%, and constrain those costs even more as workers become anxious about holding on to their jobs. As a "hard nosed" business person I face the system logic and do what makes good economic sense. Employees do not feel they have much choice so they work more, at least those who still have jobs.

Another part of the explanation comes with what Schor calls the cycle of work-and-spend. Productivity increases can translate into either decreased work time per employee or increased wages (or as we see a lot today, layoffs). Workers are rarely given the first option. They receive a small raise instead and increase their consumption, which leaves them as dependent on the existing hours as before. What makes them want to buy more when the non-monetary costs are so high?

Perhaps it has more in common with Puritan motivations than we realize. Has the Puritan's view of work as religious devotion been replaced by an economic devotion that serves the same function? God retreats but is replaced, Oz-like, by commodity standards of accomplishment and success. There are different hands behind the curtain but they are still externalized, other-directed measures of "salvation."

Additionally, the Puritan's work managed his time for him so that he would not be idle and thus susceptible to worldly temptation. As Schor makes clear, we too have managed to restrain idleness. Commodity temptation has captured us but we may be afflicted by other dangers today, for flight from unfilled time continues resolutely. Once work, shopping (at which Americans spend three to four times as much time as those in other "developed" countries), and the hours of television are deducted from our day, we are apt to be sleeping. Idle time for friends or family, civic and volunteer involvement, contemplative experience, and other such time-is-money prodigality are seriously short-shrifted. If idleness threatened damnation once upon a time, what would it threaten now? Salvation in the form of enlightenment, self-knowledge, respectful engagement with the world? Sounds odd, but what would it do to the economy if many of us converted to these practices? They are idle in a way but consumptive of potential commodity-oriented time and could threaten a turn away from the market. A system whose heart is growth and which lacks soul or moral center could not find comfort in such "salvation." It requires our full allegiance.

~

Self-suppression through work and godliness represent one side of the Puritan ethos. An equally important aspect shows up as the theme of personal transformation, often in the instant of a conversion experience, a rebirth.

I have spent some time on country roads in East Texas and the deep South, and it often appears that right after

Bible and building, however humbly constructed, rural churches find for themselves a signboard with moveable letters so new messages of inspiration and exhortation may appear regularly: "My Jesus lives. Does yours?" "Life got you down? Let Jesus pick you up." For these folk, the possibility of dramatic transformation is still very real.

Generally, though, that yearning has been appropriated by other forces. According to Jackson Lears, "ancient longings for personal transformation [became] an essential part of consumer goods' appeal in nineteenth-century America." The showmanship and elixir of the patent medicine salesman colorfully responded to the longing, but in various forms plenty of other products seduced similarly.

Lears recounts an amusing story of Herman Melville's encounter with a lightning-rod salesman in 1853 Massachusetts. The huckster appealed to surmounting anxiety, which offended Melville so much he turned the episode into a short story. According to Lears it "probed the developing mythology of market society at its most vulnerable point: the promise that people could be released from all fear and anxiety if they would simply trust in the technical expertise of the vendor."

Today product advertising not only promises relief from fear and anxiety but transformation of mundane existence's simple base metal into gold—alchemy decked out in a modern outfit. If consumerism's appropriation of that old longing for spiritual transformation reminds us of what it has done to the Christmas ritual, we should not be surprised. The dynamic of consumerism does not permit reverence or respect for anything other than its own quantitative success.

The process has an interesting rhythm. At first glance consumer culture appears to encourage excessive attachment to commodities. In reality, it encourages obsessive *preoccupation* with commodities, but could not abide attachment to anything in particular. Consumer culture understands that its average citizen already is awash with "stuff" and that daily he confronts a tsunami of appeals to buy more. The rhythm's cycle implicitly depreciates what one already has while elevating what one doesn't. We should feel dissatisfied and recognize the solution as a new commodity. There is no lasting solution, though—the phantom requires unending treatments.

It's hard to believe now, but there were times in the development of commodity culture that many worried technology could increase productivity so much that there might be insufficient demand for all its products. Gary Cross reports that in 1929 a presidential commission responded to such concerns with the pronouncement that a "New Gospel of Consumption" had thankfully emerged in America. The commission found that "wants are almost insatiable; that one want satisfied makes way for another....By advertising and other promotional devices, by scientific fact finding, and by carefully predeveloped consumption, a measurable pull on production...has been created." Relief presumably was felt by all, and the threat of underconsumption vanished from our horizons.

A variety of factors help to restrain that threat. In its seventeenth-century origins the science and technology that underlie commodity production were fueled by notions of power and control over nature's contingencies on behalf of human utility. Frequently actually useful, and certainly successful by its own measures, commodity ideology has power and offers to lend that power to those who will serve it. Further, the ideology has so captured public discourse that its premises and purposes set the terms for almost all imaginable aspiration (witness, for example, how the political realm plays handmaiden to the economy). We conform to commodity culture because most choices are defined by it. After all, what other vision of fulfillment speaks the culture so resoundingly than that of "making it"? And finally, its products—sometimes useful, usually attractively presented, always promising so much. With rich sponsors and well-paid advertisers and ubiquitous entreaties to consume, one can keep perspective only with strong will. From our point of view, the Puritans distorted spirituality. But commodity culture replaces it and infests all yearning with tangibility, with accessible marketplace versions of fulfillment.

A culture that can think of nothing better to do than work night and day to convert its citizens into wide-mouthed bottomless commodity receptacles has some reckoning to do. The merchandising mentality lands hard on people and other creatures and nature.

As I have tried to indicate in this chapter, it will not scruple to replace other aspirations, from community to spirituality, with marketplace objects and values. Part of the mechanism of consumerism lies in detaching, in experiencing othernesses as radically different and inferior: they become resources, manipulable objects, grist. Companion animals fall into this mill when they are seen as conveniences and disposables. But animals also are hunted, experimented upon, and factory-farmed. Commodification's dynamic of self-interested exploitation of the other permeates all its encounters with nonhumans, and then moves on against its progenitors' species.

A recent book speaks of the phenomenon as "wilding" and describes its occurrences ranging from random assaults to corporate malfeasance to political chicanery, much of it illegal but some simply unethical. The author considers wilding a manifestation of oversocialization to materialist and egocentric values combined with too little inhibition by moral or social codes. He considers its primary source to lie in the breakdown of connectedness—to children and family, community, nature, a larger good. If we struggle to protect the animals it is not instead of confronting other oppressions and abuses. They are all one struggle: against exploitation of the weak by those who confuse strength with superiority; against objectification; and for active recognition of the unity and community around which life should revolve.

REFERENCES

Anderson, Elizabeth. *Value in Ethics and Economics.* Cambridge: Harvard University Press, 1993.

Borgman, Albert. *Technology and the Character of Contemporary Life.* Chicago: University of Chicago Press, 1984.

Cross, Gary. *Time and Money: The Making of Consumer Culture.* New York: Routledge, 1993.

Derber, Charles. *The Wilding of America.* New York: St.

Martin's Press, 1996.

Lasch, Christopher. *The True and Only Heaven: Progress and Its Critics.* New York: W.W. Norton & Co., 1991.

Lears, Jackson. *Fables of Abundance: A Cultural History of Advertising in America.* New York: Basic Books, 1994.

Rodman, John. "The Liberation of Nature?" *Inquiry* 20 (Spring 1977).

Schor, Juliet B. *The Overworked American.* New York: Basic Books, 1991.

Weber, Max. *The Protestant Ethic and the Spirit of Capitalism.* New York: Charles Scribner's Sons, 1958.

13

INCLUSIVE ETHICS

A five-year-old boy arrives at an emergency room in the company of his mother and her boyfriend. It is not the first time but it may be the worst. An arm is broken, round pencil-sized burns dot his legs, new scars have joined the company of old, he is unconscious. The doctor looks at the child, then at his caretakers and the social worker, who leaves the treatment room to call the police. He is always so clumsy, says the mother, running into walls, pulling lamps over on himself, falling out of bed. And he bruises so easily.

Mother and boyfriend will be arrested and the child cared for in the hospital until well enough to go to relatives or a foster home. The adults may eventually face trial or they could be referred for parent education and family therapy and the boy eventually returned home. In either case he will be cared for and watched over by Children's Protective Services until they are reasonably confident of his safety.

A healthy five-year-old mixed breed dog arrives at the receiving department of an animal shelter in the company of his guardian who is moving and won't be bothered with him. By week's end the dog is dead, "euthanized" for lack of a responsible guardian or alternate home or space to keep him until one can be found.

Two creatures in distressing situations, one abused and the other neglected, their outcomes dramatically different (although both have arrived at this unfortunate juncture due to the perpetrators' shared disregard for another's welfare). Many would consider the child's subsequent protection and the dog's destruction to be normal and appropriate and think the comparison like apples to oranges. In this view a child's life is patently more valuable than a dog's. But if so, what makes it that way? Of what is the greater value constituted? How can we compare the relative value of lives between individuals or species?

Researchers who use animals in their experiments are accused of an inconsistency. They say animals are so different from humans that they do not deserve comparable moral consideration for their welfare. Then they say animals are so like humans that research results using them are valuably applicable to understanding what's good for *our* welfare. So very different yet so very similar. And as if arranged by Providence the respective qualities conveniently lie where the objective, value-free researcher would have wanted them.

One will search long and hard before finding a credible scientist who would deny evolution as the best explanation of biological development over the eons. "Creationist" interpretations favored by religious enthusiasts merit hardly a footnote. Yet the scientists' "very different" dogma bespeaks a kind of Special Creation notion of human genesis which the religious enthusiasts might well applaud. Presumably the sacrality, or whatever phlogiston-like substance it is, that uniquely elevates human beings above all other creation erupted in a quantum leap—Special Evolutionary Creation.

Philosophers and others propose a host of distinctions between humans and other animals to justify the very different ways we typically treat them. Self-consciousness, rationality, language, moral agency, possession of a soul—an abundant variety of such qualities are supposed to set us apart and above other creatures. But these arguments cannot succeed because of the problem of marginal cases such as infants or the demented or profoundly retarded who lack the necessary qualification for moral priority but are granted it anyway. Or the arguments are arbitrary: how does possession of human-type rationality, for example, engender higher moral value? Our kind of rationality is useful in our kind of lives, but its connection with moral importance remains mysterious. What about those who possess rationality but who fail to use it or use it for evil ends? Despite these problems and others, the presumption of inherent human moral superiority dominates most people's view of the human place in the world. If these characteristically human qualities fail to justify claims to superiority, what other reasons are there?

Habit, history, and social reinforcement along with perceptions of self-interest are part of it. Humans are accustomed to thinking this way, and we are powerfully preoccupied with self. Also, tribalism pervades relations between humans. It may similarly put a gap between us and other species due in part to prejudice and natural affinity for those biologically closest to us. Intra-species identification and empathy will exceed that between us and other species. Could it be otherwise—could we ever be as reliably and fully receptive to a nonhuman as to one of our kind?

All these things will help to explain our preference for our own species, but they are not morally compelling reasons for doing so. In their malignant forms they can as well rationalize racism as speciesism. They offer psychological illumination of characteristic human behaviors without establishing justifications for them. In his history of the idea of the "great chain of being" Arthur Lovejoy noted that among those in much earlier times who thought about the seemingly vast distance between the lives of toads and humans there were some who surmised that that was still very little compared to the distance between humans and God. Pondering that, they found humility an appropriate virtue. But not in our time.

Weighing the comparative value of lives would surely offend us if the lives involved were solely those of humans. If you are making a decision about an organ transplant, say, and have only one organ but many patients, procedures for allocating the surgery become necessary: age, health, prognosis, etc. Discriminatory treatment is acceptable when unavoidable and based on nonarbitrary criteria. We assume that the patients are equal morally but still we must make a choice. In short, necessity is the mother of ranking criteria which in its absence we eschew, and properly so. Our moral burden is to find alternatives to such tragic choices whenever we can.

When we abandon the assumption of inevitable human priority, things change crucially. In particular, the central question for an ethical community becomes how to promote the good for *life*, rather than just human life. Less expansively, how can we pursue our good in the manner most respectful and least damaging to the larger good? Thinking about companion animals, for example, what do we owe them, what can we offer them in lieu of a painless death at the animal shelter?

When one considers ethical theories, particularly human-centered ones (and most are), or listens to people's everyday justifications of questionable behavior, it is easy to picture corporate lawyers searching for loopholes in IRS tax codes. What can be gotten away with? Who or what can be excluded from consideration? How can I have my moral cake while consuming its substance?

But the spirit of ethics opposes this approach. It wants to be inclusive rather than miserly, visionary rather than legalistic. Its spirit challenges: Why not more rather than fewer on our horizon of care?

Approaches to Ethics

This section brings together a variety of threads from which an embracing fabric for ethical engagement with animals can be sewn. It recognizes the importance of unending dialogue between reason and experience, needs of individuals and those of communities, and between approaches to the Good. Its conception of an inclusive ethic implicates both the range of existing life and the range of considerations in expressing appropriate ethical concern.

The first and very well known modern thread came from Peter Singer with the publication of *Animal Liberation* in 1975. He approaches the question from a utilitarian perspective. To begin with, in an effort to resolve differences between groups or to determine what is best for a particular group the only relevant criteria are the interests of the members. Race, gender, ethnicity, species, or other such considerations are germane only insofar as they are shown to be non-arbitrarily connected to those interests. Second, "The capacity for suffering and enjoyment is, however, not only necessary, but also sufficient for us to say that a being has interests—at an absolute minimum, an interest in not suffering." Third, every sentient creature deserves equal consideration of its interests. This does not mean equal treatment or equal "rights" necessarily, for that is a function of the nature of its interests. When we concern ourselves in this way with the suffering of different creatures, we see that suffering is suffering. There is no validity in treating it as evil among humans but acceptable for members of other species. So this perspective concerns itself with the "greatest good" of all sentient creatures related to how much they suffer or prosper in their relations with humans.

Tom Regan presents another approach, one that also appeals to a vision of equality but in this case of inherent value. Inherent value of individual lives refers to their "having value in themselves" apart from the value of their experiences or their personal characteristics or value to others. It is unearned and invariable and equal among all who have it. And those who have it must share some relevant similarity, one of which Regan conceives as their being the "subject-of-a-life." Such subjects have a collection of characteristics: beliefs, desires, perception, memory, a sense of the future, emotions, sensations, initiative, identity, and an individual welfare in the sense that things can go better or worse for them. Along with humans many other animals have these characteristics to varying degrees and thus are subjects-of-a-life with equal inherent value. For these individuals "any principle that declares what treatment is due them as a matter of justice must take their equal value into account. The following principle (the respect principle) does this: We are to treat those individuals who have inherent value in ways that respect their inherent value." This principle recognizes a basic moral right of such beings and requires that they not be harmed and that they be assisted if they suffer injustice.

Utilitarians (such as Singer) and rights adherents (such as Regan) controvert one another in a variety of areas, but that is not a present concern. Each addresses facets of ani-

mal needs or claims in relation to humans that are important. Singer and Regan are careful to define the boundaries
for application of their ethical concerns: sentience and subject-of-a-life. Both, it seems to me, exhibit obvious good sense
and compassion. Without concern for suffering or for inherent value, an ethic for our relations with the animals could
hardly be responsive to their needs and well-being. Even so,
emphasis on possession of traits and their implications does
not adequately capture what happens when we respond ethically to fellow creatures.

Paul Taylor reaches farther. In 1986 he wrote *Respect for
Nature* to explore a question: "What is the ethical significance of our being members of the Earth's Community of
Life?" In answer he proposed a biocentric outlook on nature
consisting of four beliefs.

First, humans are members of the community on the
same terms as other life. We, too, are biological creatures
with corresponding requirements to survive and do well in a
world not altogether under our control. Although humans
enjoy greater autonomy in choosing a life course, all that
lives depends on an absence of artificial and unnecessarily
imposed constraints to realize the unique possibilities of its
existence. Like other creatures, humans are products of evolution, quite recent products in fact, who could never have
appeared and survived without the preexisting fabric of life.
And while the biosphere would not suffer in the least from
human extinction (would benefit, actually), its healthfulness
and stability rely utterly on the activity of countless other
species.

The second belief of the biocentric outlook is that humans share with the rest of life an ecological interdepen-
dence on the good and more or less harmonious functioning
of other parts of the whole. We inhabit a web of life, and to
our apparent disappointment and embarrassment we do not
and cannot survive without it.

Third, all individual organisms have their unique, spe-
cies-specific ways of being, maintaining themselves, repro-
ducing, and fulfilling their possibilities. That is, they have a
good of their own the realization of which is better than its
not being realized. Based on this, they have inherent worth,

a worth irrespective of their value to or for any other purpose. If permitted, every form of life develops in ways and
directions that from its perspective are good. *Being* is its
own justification and its own value.

Following on these three beliefs, and most important of
all, the biocentric outlook rejects the common notion of human superiority over the rest of creation. According to Taylor there are no good (nonarbitrary, defensible) reasons to
accept the idea of human superiority, and he refutes four
candidate attempts to convince us otherwise. These are 1)
the classical Greek view based on human possession of reason; 2) traditional Christian views derived from Great Chain
of Being portrayals of human elevation over other creation
and proximity to God; 3) Cartesian assertions of a human
monopoly of mind; and 4) versions of superior human inherent worth that rest on our possession of a greater range
of capacities than other creatures. A variety of considerations argue against these defenses of human superiority,
and they fail because they rely on non sequitur, bias, and
arbitrary associations of certain qualities with degrees of
worth.

What do reason, mind, and other such capacities have
to do with inherent worth? Think what our response would
be (and regarding certain historical events *is* in our response
to fascist declarations about "life unworthy of life") to the
application of such logic to differentiate degrees of worth
among humans. How much worthier is Jane because of her
greater capacities and reasoning abilities than Joe with his
relatively inferior ones? If having "x" makes one superior to
those supposedly without it, does having more of "x" make
one morally superior to those with less?

The upshot of the biocentric perspective, says Taylor, is
this:

> If we view the realm of nature and life from the per-
> spective of the first three elements of the
> biocentric outlook, we will see ourselves as
> having a deep kinship with all other living things,
> sharing with them many common characteristics and
> being, like them, integral parts of one great whole
> encompassing the natural order of life on our planet.

>When we focus on the reality of their individual lives, we see each one to be in many ways like ourselves, responding in its particular manner to environmental circumstances and so pursuing the realization of its own good. It is within the framework of this conceptual system that the idea of human superiority is found to be unreasonable....We come to see how all that gives meaning to human existence is made possible by the surrounding conditions of life and nature....Our oneness with all the other members of the great Community of Life is acknowledged and confirmed.

Taylor presents his ideas in the form of philosophic argument, but they clearly represent profound dialogue between conceptualizing and experiencing. Central to the ethic is this: "We can now understand how it is possible for a human being to take an animal's standpoint and, without a trace of anthropomorphism, make a factually informed and objective judgment regarding what is desirable or undesirable from that standpoint." In exercising that judgment we recognize obligations that, as with Regan, reflect an attitude of respect. These include duties not to harm or interfere with others in the absence of vital needs, and of restitutive justice when harm or injustice have been inflicted.

Taylor's description of biological reality in the first three beliefs of the biocentric outlook is persuasive, but many will have a hard time with the move from there to species-impartiality based on equal inherent worth of humans and other creatures. That movement may not come at all unless one enters into relationships with other life equipped equally with reason and emotional receptivity. Taylor speaks of it as the expression of character, that is, the disposition to deliberate rationally and clearly combined with the will to act even when it entails sacrifice: "a power of self-mastery and self-control that gives one the strength of will to meet one's responsibilities." And speaking of character introduces the ancient conception of the virtues, those traits that embody and express excellence of character.

He divides these between general and special virtues, and the former further between those of moral strength and moral concern. The notion of concern expresses the idea of relationship as the chrysalis of right action. It stresses the willingness "to take the standpoint of animals and plants" as the foundation and motivation for respect and includes the virtues of benevolence, compassion, sympathy, and caring. Moral strength enables concern to meet the demands of duty and includes such virtues as conscientiousness, integrity, patience, courage, disinterestedness, and perseverance. The special virtues, finally, are those on which specific duties depend, for example, considerateness underlies the duty of nonharm and impartiality does the same for noninterference.

Our ethical engagement with animals becomes more inclusive with each of these steps: from a concern with suffering to respect for the inherent value of subjects-of-a-life and then to respect for the inherent worth of nature as a whole. The final step moved to the virtues on which all of the other steps depend for genesis and execution and leads us to the linkage between the object of ethical consideration and the subject who does the considering.

I now arrive at another perspective with its own contribution to a more inclusive ethic. The notion of *care* as a distinctive form of moral reasoning and behavior began with the work of Carol Gilligan as reported in *In a Different Voice* about a decade and a half ago. As she studied the psychology of moral development she noticed that two "voices" seemed to differentiate males and females. The former tended to speak in terms of justice, equality, and individual rights and duties. The latter she described as expressing concerns for care and responsibility, empathy and relationship. Her work sparked considerable interest and controversy and spawned a significant body of writings on feminist ethics. I depend chiefly on Gilligan and on Virginia Held's anthology, *Justice and Care*, in what follows.

What is care as an ethic as opposed to just a feeling or a sentiment? Held, in her own essay for the book, speaks of feminist morality as concerned to move beyond knowledge and improved practices "to cultivate the art of living a life." As an ethic, caring involves a unity of oneself centered around care and its companion assumptions and attitudes.

Caring sentiment at its best becomes an episode within caring existence.

How does it develop? The natural history of a care ethic, according to Nel Noddings, incorporates a two-part, or two feelings, process. It begins in "natural caring," the nearly universal experience of being moved by the presence or needs of another. Without emotions like this there can be no ethic, but at most conformity or self-interested artifice. The second part consists of the movement from caring as *natural* to caring as *mandate* and arises from our best memories of ourselves caring and being cared for. The feelings from those moments, along with a vision of an ideal ethical self, thus emerge as "I must."

Relatedness provides the fertile soil in which a care ethic is rooted and nourished. The ethic assumes that relatedness establishes valuable life and that a life's texture varies according to relation's quality. In Noddings' words, "this strong desire to be moral is derived, reflectively, from the more fundamental and natural desire to be and to remain related....the genuine moral sentiment...arises from an evaluation of the caring relation as good, as better than, superior to, other forms of relatedness....The source of my obligation is the value I place on the relatedness of caring." On behalf of that ideal ethical self, "I care about myself as one caring."

These are important ideas worth reiteration. She asserts certain universal realities: caring is a natural, innate sentiment; valuable forms of being are founded on relation; caring relation is superior to any other. If one wishes to flourish—and who does not?—one's orientation will be around the centering ideal of oneself caring. I realize personal completeness, she says, chiefly in caring relation.

A variety of attitudes and behaviors characterize an ethic of caring: dialogical communication (address and response), attentiveness, receptivity, connection, general and particular knowledge. Embodied in the caring one, expressed as her living, all these aspects underlie the ethic in action.

Two final observations. Noddings has problems with the application of her ideas to relations with animals. She believes our obligations toward them are weakened by the fact that the reciprocity is unbalanced. While I recognize that mutuality in relations with animals takes different forms than among ourselves and that completeness and equitability are limited by inherent species differences, I think she forgets that as in our relations with dependents, the adult human can express care as fully as she wills to give herself to the relation. We do not expect equitable reciprocity, but as we behold the child or the wild or companion animal we receive what they have to give, each in its own way, and that suffices.

Second, although an ethic of care is natural and desirable, there is no sure proof against its perversion or suppression. So much seems to hinge on early experiences of care, so that the seeds may germinate and grow to destined good, that we easily can imagine how distortions of the caring/relating impulse onto false objects or self-preoccupations may abort it. Caring ones must make every effort to help a caring environment flourish.

Views on Ethical Relatedness

The ethic set out in these pages intends to be inclusive: it wants to prevent and abate suffering when called upon, to respect the inherent value of all life, to encourage development of character through insemination of the moral virtues, to culminate in people striving for responsible, caring relatedness with that part of the world which comes to their attention or which they might affect. It assumes that the world of nature, including humans and the other animals, "speaks" intelligibly to one who cares to listen, and that it sometimes needs our active engagement and other times the respect of noninterference. Nature unfolds toward her own fine purposes, as does the listener toward hers, and part of an ethic's task is to manage conflicts among those purposes, for each being is intrinsically valuable.

Thinking about forms of relatedness seems as important as anything in all this. The narrative of a human's life may be as much defined by his characteristic patterns of relation as by anything: engaged or detached, receptive or closed, caring or indifferent. When the world speaks, these determine how we listen and respond.

Hans Jonas describes a law: "the appeal of a possible

good-in-itself in the world, which confronts my will and demands to be heard...is precisely what the moral law commands: this law is nothing but the general enjoinder of the call of all action-dependent 'goods' and of their situation-determined right to just my action." In other words, the world does in fact speak and we must listen (as we wish to be listened to) and respond justly and caringly. Jonas believes we recognize the law's validity through the emotions, chiefly the feeling of responsibility (or care, as the others put it above). We can respond, and we respond as ones accountable for how it goes with the other insofar as we act in ways that affect it.

Jonas' law seems more like a principle of nature than an artificially imposed rule, for we are fundamentally beings-in-relation. For Martin Buber, too, the essence of human existence lies in mutuality between self and other: "He who takes his stand in relation shares in a reality, that is, in a being that neither merely belongs to him nor merely lies outside him. All reality is an activity in which I share without being able to appropriate for myself. Where there is no sharing there is no reality." But as we recognized above regarding the vulnerability of caring to subversion by other purposes and ways, mutuality of relation is endangered by preoccupation with overly self-interested strivings; we "flee to the possessing of things before the unreliable, perilous world of relation" which is intangible and less controllable. Buber continues:

> The self-willed man does not believe...and does not know solidarity of connexion [sic], but only the feverish world outside and his feverish desire to use it. Use needs only to be given an ancient name, and it companies with the gods. When this man says Thou, he means "O my ability to use," and what he terms his destiny is only the equipping and sanctioning of his ability to use. He has in truth...only a being that is defined by things and instincts, which he fulfills with the feeling of sovereignty.

For Buber, such being as this contradicts and defeats itself, for one has a natural inclination and need for engaged relation. That "feeling of sovereignty" of the egoist arises as a marketplace artifact, a means with no end but itself.

Conclusion

Thinking back to the boy and the dog that began this essay, it seems clear that their shared need was for connection with another who experienced a sense of responsibility for their welfare. Parents and companions to animals who are sunk into self-preoccupation have denied or dissolved the relation they chose and the obligation of it. They are damaged or irresponsible and are unable or unwilling to see beyond themselves. They reflect prototypical characteristics of personalities generated by commodity culture.

I wanted to bring together the strands of ethical conception represented in the preceding for at least two reasons. First, each focuses on a vital part of what it means to live toward the ethical good, and unified they help to complete and strengthen that effort. Culminating in the notions of respect, care, responsibility, and relational mutuality they also reflect a more nearly seamless ethic, one having as much to do with the kind of person one is as with his beliefs. Second, to emphasize an inclusive and connected world helps to counter the dominant disturbance of our time which lies in self-absorption and bonds that are fragmented. Each of these considerations supports the cause of animal protection.

The picture of biocentric entwinement drawn by Paul Taylor shows biological reality; evolution and ecology lift the mask of our pretense to human separateness and autonomy. More receptive natures than ours might find moral guidance and gratitude in the truth that we are dependent on the whole. Biological continuity suggests as well other forms of connection: spiritual, communitarian, diversity within the structure of unity. Nature at large offers abundant evidence of her delight in *life*, and maybe she hoped with humans to complement that with a consciousness that would take equal pleasure in *lives*. Early peoples may have done that, but the modern obsession with individualistic goals tends to negate the inherent values of both. We need to reopen this question of the self in relation to others. And we must realize the proper privileges and responsibilities of our unique kind among our fellow species.

REFERENCES

Buber, Martin. *Between Man and Man.* New York: Collier Books, 1965.

———. *I and Thou.* New York: Charles Scribner's Sons, 1958.

Gilligan, Carol. *In a Different Voice.* Cambridge: Harvard University Press, 1982.

Held, Virginia (ed.). *Justice and Care: Essential Readings in Feminist Ethics.* Boulder: Westview Press, 1995.

Jonas, Hans. *The Imperative of Responsibility.* Chicago: University of Chicago Press, 1984.

Miller, Harlan & William Williams (ed.). *Ethics and Animals.* Clifton, NJ: Humana Press, 1983.

Regan, Tom. *The Case for Animal Rights.* Berkeley: University of California Press, 1983.

Singer, Peter. *Animal Liberation.* New York: Avon Books, 1990, Revised Edition.

Taylor, Paul. *Respect for Nature: A Theory of Environmental Ethics.* Princeton: Princeton University Press, 1986.

APPENDIX

For readers who want more information about how welfare and advocacy organizations nationally and regionally are responding to some of the dangers faced by animals, I offer the following sample (in their own words). If you are like many who commit themselves to increasing the respect with which animals are treated, you will join a national group (or two or three) with whose goals you identify and become involved locally as well. For the latter, check the yellow page listing under "animal shelters" and be aware through your newspaper of meetings and other activities of activists in your area. If companion animals are your strongest interest, look for humane societies, SPCAs, and animal control; visit, ask questions, get involved. The animals will appreciate it.

American Humane Association
63 Inverness Drive East
Englewood, Colorado 80112
(303)792-9900   fax 792-5333
e-mail: amerhumane@aol.com
Contact: Animal Protection Division
Mission: Preventing neglect, abuse, and exploitation of animals and children. The Animal Protection Division seeks to end animal cruelty and suffering by tackling issues for all animals' well-being. Pet overpopulation is the main thrust of AHA's work. AHA assists animal shelters across the nation, rescues animals during natural disasters, provides humane education, protects animals in film and advocates on legislative issues locally and in Washington, D.C.

Animal Protection Institute of America (API)

P.O. Box 22505
Sacramento, CA 95822
(916)731-5521   fax 731-4467
(800)348-7387
Contact: Alan H. Berger, Executive Director

Mission: API is a nonprofit advocacy organization formed in 1968 with 75,000 members nationwide. API is dedicated to protecting animals against abuse through enforcement/legislative actions, investigations, advocacy campaigns, crisis intervention, public awareness, and education. Specific areas of concern are wildlife protection/habitat conservation, companion animals, marine mammals, domestic/farm animals, animals used in research, and humane education.

Animal Rights Mobilization (ARM!)

P.O. Box 6989
Denver, CO 80206-6989
(303)388-7120   fax 388-7182
Contact: Robin Duxbury, Director

Mission: ARM! (formerly Trans-Species Unlimited) is a national, grassroots networking organization with affiliated local groups in cities and towns across the country. It is dedicated to the elimination of animal abuse and exploitation of all non-human animal species. ARM! has four divisions: Information and Research, Education & Outreach, Campaigns, and Networking. ARM! is the founding organization of the Campaign for a *Fur-Free America*™ and *Fur-Free Friday*™, a national day of protest against the killing of animals for fur. ARM! has successfully campaigned against the captivity of marine mammals, the eradication of the decompression chamber, and animal research. ARM! is the only national animal rights organization that is all-volunteer, and does not employ any professional fund-raisers.

Animal Welfare Institute

P.O. Box 3650
Washington, D.C. 20007
(202)337-2332   fax 338-9478
e-mail: awi@animalwelfare.com

Contact: Jenny Pike (re membership)

Mission: AWI was founded in 1951 to reduce the suffering, pain, and fear inflicted on animals by humans. AWI is a research and educational organization, publishing books and pamphlets which are distributed free on request to libraries, schools, universities, chiefs of police, and humane societies, or sold at cost. Primary concerns include factory farming, cruel trapping devices, preservation of whales and other endangered species, capture of exotic birds for the commercial pet trade, and mistreatment of laboratory animals. AWI members receive a subscription to the *AWI Quarterly*, which features animal welfare news, reports by undercover investigators, and guidelines for letter writing campaigns.

The Animals' Agenda

P.O. Box 25881
Baltimore, MD 21224
(410)675-4566   fax 675-0066
e-mail: office@animalsagenda.org
www.animalsagenda.org
Contact: Kirsten Rosenberg, Managing Editor

Mission: *The Animals' Agenda* is a bimonthly magazine dedicated to informing people about animal rights and cruelty-free living for the purpose of inspiring action for animals. *The Animals' Agenda* is committed to serving—and fostering cooperation among—a combined audience of animal advocates, interested individuals, and the entire animal rights movement. Each issue includes investigative reports, in-depth analysis of topical issues, news briefs, feature articles on key animal rights issues, commentary, reviews, "Your Agenda" (practical action you can take), and an annual directory of animal advocacy organizations, an indispensable tool for all animal advocates!

Associated Humane Societies

Humane Way—Box 43
Forked River, NJ 08731
(609)693-1900   fax 693-8404
Contact: Roseann Trezza, Assistant Director

Mission: The object of the Associated Humane Societies, Inc. shall be the prevention of cruelty to animals throughout the U.S. and specifically the State of New Jersey, maintenance of animal care centers, proper appliances for disposal of sick, injured and abandoned animals which shall include crematorium and hospital, the maintenance of a hospital clinic and other facilities for the care, treatment and disposition of sick and injured animals, to educate and instruct the public in the care and treatment of animals and to encourage humane education in public and private schools and to do whatever is necessary to promote the general welfare of animals everywhere.

Compassion Campaign for Animals
P.O. Box 52193
Philadelphia, PA 19115
(215)396-2587   fax 396-2516
Contact: Paula Wilson

Mission: Our organization is devoted to educating the public about the unnecessary cruel testing of animals that the Beauty, Personal Care and Fashion industries undertake before introducing their products to the market, as well as informing the public about which companies have stopped testing and which companies continue to test. Our International Spokesperson is international model/actress Maria Liberati.

Doing Things for Animals, Inc. (DTFA)
P.O. Box 2165
Sun City, AZ 85372-2165
Phone/fax (602)977-5793
e-mail: FORODTFA@ix.netcom.com
Contact: Lynda J. Foro, President

Mission: DTFA advocates for communication and support among humane organizations. Believing that animal caregivers have more in common than separates them, DTFA provides networking resources to enhance the opportunities for groups to work together. These tools include publishing the *No-Kill Directory* and hosting the "No Kills in the '90s" conference each year. DTFA offers consultation services in nonprofit management to smaller humane organizations. DTFA works nationally to promote respect and recognition for the diversity in animal welfare. Founder Lynda Foro welcomes opportunities to speak on the future of the humane movement.

Doris Day Animal League

Suite 100
227 Massachusetts Avenue, N.E.
Washington, D.C. 20002
(202)546-1761   fax 546-2193
e-mail: ddal@aol.com
Contact: Bonnie Smith

Mission: The Doris Day Animal League's overriding mission is to reduce the pain and suffering of non-human animals, encourage the spaying and neutering of companion animals, and increase the public's awareness of its responsibility toward non-human animals through legislative initiatives, public education, and programs to require the enforcement of statutes and regulations that have already been enacted to protect animals.

Farm Animal Reform Movement (FARM)

P.O. Box 30654
Bethesda, MD 20824
(301)530-1737   fax 530-5747
(800)MEATOUT   (888)ASK FARM
e-mail: FARM@gnn.com
Contact: Beth Fiteni

Mission: Founded in 1981, FARM is the oldest animal rights organization devoted entirely to exposing and eliminating animal abuse and other destructive impacts of intensive animal agriculture. FARM works with local groups and activists around the world in conducting high-profile campaigns like the Great American Meatout (March 20), National Veal Ban Action (Mother's Day), World Farm Animals Day (October 2), and CHOICE (Consumers for Healthy Options in Children's Education).

Farm Sanctuary

P.O. Box 150   Box 1065
Watkins Glen, NY 14891   Orland, CA 95963
(607)583-2225   (916)865-4617
http://www.farmsanctuary.org
Contact: Holly McNulty

Mission: Since 1986 Farm Sanctuary has been directly rescuing farm animals and initiating campaigns to stop farm animal abuses by operating the largest shelters in the country for victims of "food animal" production; successfully prosecuting stockyards and factory farms for cruelty to farm animals; passing the first state legislation to ban "downed" animal abuses at stockyards and slaughterhouses; and national news exposes and public education programs. Write or call for a free copy of our latest newsletter to find out what YOU can do to help farm animals.

Hooved Animal Humane Society

P.O. Box 400
Woodstock, Illinois 60098
(815)337-5563   fax 337-5569
e-mail: smeiler@aol.com

Mission: The Hooved Animal Humane Society was founded in 1971 after Donna Ewing was searching for a horse for her daughter. What she found was shocking—a herd of Arabian horses in various stages of malnutrition. After contacting everyone from local police to animal control, she found that nobody had the authority or ability to help. Today, thanks to HAHS and its supporters there is hope and help. Here's how: Cruelty investigations, rescue of suffering animals, humane care, legislation, and education.

The Humane Coalition of Massachusetts, Inc.

P.O. Box 551
Mansfield, MA 02048-0551
(617)344-3874
Contact: Bonney Brown, Secretary

Mission: To promote networking among alternative humane organizations: no-kill animal shelters, low cost spay/neuter clinics, canine breed rescue groups, animal protection organizations, wildlife rehabilitators and feral cats trap-neuter-release programs. To assist these organizations in achieving their individual goals by providing information and referrals and to work together to effectively achieve common goals.

In Defense of Animals
131 Camino Alto, Suite E
Mill Valley, CA 94941
(415)388-9641   fax 388-0388
e-mail: IDA@well.com
Contact: Emma Clifford

Mission: Founded in 1983 by veterinarian Elliot M. Katz, IDA is a leading, national, nonprofit organization dedicated to ending the institutionalized exploitation and abuse of animals by defending their rights, welfare, and habitat. IDA is committed to ending the terror of animal maltreatment, and educating the public about the benefits of compassion. IDA is pro-science, pro-environment, pro-animal, and pro-people; it is committed to dialogue and reason, but not afraid to take action when necessary to save animals from senseless torture. IDA has more than 70,000 members and a dedicated staff with diverse experience in science, medicine, politics, community organizing, and public relations. Now, more than ever, IDA is a force for desperately needed change.

International Fund for Animal Welfare
411 Main St.
Yarmouth Port, MA 02675
(508)362-2649   fax 362-5841
Contact: Karen Butler, Membership and Kristina Hemenway, Program Information

Mission: The major areas of concentration for IFAW in early 1997 are the Canadian seal hunt, anti-whaling, bear bile farms in China, fox hunting in England, African elephants, animal emergency relief, and the Pet Rescue Grant Project for no-kill animal protection groups.

International Society for Animal Rights, Inc.
421 South State Street

Clarks Summit, PA 18411
(717)586-2200   fax 586-9580

Mission: ISAR believes that because of their sentient nature, animals have rights, rights that are denied them in law and daily life. Animals share more than the planet with humans. Like us, they are capable of knowing pain, fear, and other suffering. ISAR, the first organization in the world to use the term Animal Rights in a corporate name, works to expose and seeks to end the injustice of the exploitation of animals and the suffering inflicted on them. There's a commitment in ISAR's name: to bring about rights for animals, the right not to be made victims because they are weak and defenseless. ISAR addresses itself to finding out why and how animals are victimized and then developing strategy to redress the wrong. ISAR doesn't believe in applying Band-Aids to mortal wounds. The Society seeks to end, rather than to regulate, uses of animals that deny their rights and cause them suffering.

Jews for Animal Rights/JAR
255 Humphrey Street
Marblehead, MA 01945
(617)631-7601   fax 639-0772
e-mail: micah@micahbooks.com
Contact: Robert or Roberta Kalechofsky

Mission: JAR works to end cruelty towards animals and a more respectful attitude of the human race toward non-human creatures. We promote vegetarianism, the insights of preventative medicine, alternatives to animal research, community action programs, discussion groups, educational programs, newsletters, speakers, videos and publications. We can advise on social action programs and themes for bar/bat mitzvah or confirmation talks. Micah publications is the publishing arm for JAR and can be contacted through http:www.micahbooks.com.

The Latham Foundation
Latham Plaza Building, Clement & Schiller
Alameda, CA 94501
(510)521-0920   fax 521-9861

e-mail: LATHM@AOL.COM ~ htt://www.latham.org./
Contact: Hugh H. Tebault, President

Mission: To promote, foster, encourage and further the principles of humaneness, kindness and benevolence to all living creatures; the doctrines of universal brotherhood and justice; the prevention and eradication of cruelty to animals and all living creatures, with particular emphasis on the education of children in justice and kindness to animals.

Massachusetts Society for the Prevention of Cruelty to Animals/American Humane Education Society
350 So. Huntington Avenue
Boston, MA 02130
(617)522-7400   fax 522-4885
Contact: Nancy Harding, Director of Membership

Mission: The mission of the MSPCA/AHES is to protect animals, relieve their suffering, advance their welfare, prevent cruelty, and work for a just and compassionate society. We provide a wider range of services than any other animal-protection organization in the nation. These include public and classroom education, legislative advocacy, seven small-animal shelters, a law enforcement unit, emergency rescue operations, a large-animal shelter, the Center for Laboratory Animal Welfare, and three animal hospitals, including the world-renowned Angell Memorial Animal Hospital. The MSPCA/AHES strives to promote justice for all living creatures.

National Anti-Vivisection Society (NAVS)
53 West Jackson Blvd.
Chicago, Illinois 60604-3795
(312)427-6065   fax 427-6524
(800)888-NAVS   (800)922-FROG (dissection hotline)
e-mail: navs@navs.org ~ http://www.navs.org.

Mission: The National Anti-Vivisection Society is dedicated to abolishing the exploitation of animals used in research, education and product testing. NAVS promotes greater compassion, respect, and justice for animals through educational programs based on respected ethical and scientific theory and supported by extensive documentation of the cruelty and waste of vivisection. NAVS' educational programs are directed at increasing public awareness about vivisection, identifying humane solutions to human problems, developing alternatives to the use of animals and working with like-minded individuals and groups to effect changes which help to end suffering inflicted on innocent animals.

People for the Ethical Treatment of Animals
501 Front St.
Norfolk, VA 23510
(757)622-7382   fax 622-0457
e-mail: PETA@Norfolk.infi.net
Contact: Karen Johnson (ext. 306)

Mission: PETA is an international nonprofit organization. Founded in 1980, PETA is dedicated to establishing and defending the rights of all animals and operates under the simple principle that animals are not ours to eat, wear, experiment on, or use for entertainment. PETA's animal protection work brings together members of the scientific, judicial, and legislative communities to halt abusive practices. Numerous PETA cases, aided by thorough investigative work, congressional involvement, consumer boycotts, and international media coverage, resulted in long-term changes that have improved the quality of life for, and prevented the deaths of, many thousands of animals.

Psychologists for the Ethical Treatment of Animals
P.O. Box 1297
Washington Grove, MD 20880-1297
(240)963-4751   fax 963-4751
e-mail: kshapiro@capaccess.org
http//index.html ~ www.psyeta.org
Contact: Susan Burt

Mission: **PSY**ETA is a non-profit organization comprised of psychologists working in cooperation with other professional and animal rights organizations to change the way individuals and society as a whole treat non-human animals. The psychologists who make up our board and membership work in academic, clinical, community and research settings worldwide. We are dedicated to the enrichment and protection of both human and non-human lives, and believe this can only occur via the strengthening of a humane ethical basis for our attitudes, feelings, behaviors and interactions. We support all people who strive to enhance human compassion and to enrich the world via respect not only for each other, but for all non-human animals as well.

United Humanitarians

P.O. Box 14587
Philadelphia, PA 19115
(215)750-0171
Contact: Adele P. Hudson, Executive V.P.

Mission: United Humanitarians was chartered in California in 1969 as a nonprofit anti-cruelty organization. One of our major thrusts is the mass sterilization of owners' pet dogs and cats through low cost spaying and neutering. This program is carried on by United Humanitarian branches located throughout the United States, with the generous cooperation of participating veterinarians. We have been responsible for the sterilization of millions of dogs and cats. By preventing the births of untold numbers of puppies and kittens for which there are no homes available an incalculable amount of suffering has been prevented.

United Poultry Concerns, Inc.

P.O. Box 59367
Potomac, Maryland 20859
(301)948-2406   fax 948-2406
www.envirolink.org/arrs/upc
Contact: Karen Davis, President

Mission: United Poultry Concerns is a nonprofit organization which addresses the treatment of domestic fowl in food production, science, education, entertainment, and human companionship situations. We promote the compassionate and respectful treatment of domestic fowl and a vegan lifestyle through research and investigations and vigorous public education campaigns. Programs include alternatives to chick-hatching projects and campaigns against battery cages for laying hens. We maintain a chicken sanctuary. We publish a quarterly newsletter, *PoultryPress.* KarenDavis, PhD, President is the author of *Prisoned Chickens, Poisoned Eggs: An Inside Look at the Modern Poultry Industry* (The Book Publishing Company, 1996).

BIBLIOGRAPHY

Adams, Carol. *The Sexual Politics of Meat.* New York: Continuum, 1990.

Adas, Michael. *Machines as the Measure of Men.* Ithica: Cornell University Press, 1989.

Anchel, Marjorie (ed.). *Overpopulation of Cats and Dogs: Causes, Effects, and Prevention.* New York: Fordham University Press, 1990.

Anderson, Elizabeth. *Value in Ethics and Economics.* Cambridge: Harvard University Press, 1993.

Arluke, Arnold. "Coping With Euthanasia: A Case Study of Shelter Culture." *JAVMA,* Vol. 198, #7, pp. 1176-1180.

Berry, Wendell. *What Are People For?* San Francisco: North Point Press, 1990.

Borgman, Albert. *Technology and the Character of Contemporary Life.* Chicago: University of Chicago Press, 1984.

Buber, Martin. *I and Thou.* New York: Charles Scribner's Sons, 1958.

———. *Between Man and Man.* New York: Collier Books, 1965.

Callahan, Daniel. *The Troubled Dream of Life.* New York: Simon & Schuster, 1993.

Causey, Ann S. "On the Morality of Hunting." *Environmental Ethics,* Vol. 11, No. 4, (Winter 1989), pp. 327-343.

Coleman, Sydney H. *Humane Society Leaders in America.* New York: American Humane Association, 1924.

Cook, E.T. & A. Wedderburn (eds.). *The Works of John Ruskin.* London: George Allen, 1904. Vols. I & V.

Cross, Gary. *Time and Money: The Making of Consumer Culture.* New York: Routledge, 1993.

Derber, Charles. *The Wilding of America.* New York: St. Martin's Press, 1996.

Dominico, Terry & Mark Newman. *Bears of the World.* New York: Facts On File, 1988.

BIBLIOGRAPHY

Donald, Rhonda Lucas. "The No-Kill Controversy." *Shelter Sense*, September 1991, pp. 3-6.

Duvin, Ed. "In the Name of Mercy." *animalines*, Vol. 4, #11.

———. "Benign Neglect." *animalines*, Vol. 4, #12.

Elshtain, Jean Bethke (ed.). *Just War Theory*. Washington Square: New York University Press, 1992.

Gilligan, Carol. *In a Different Voice*. Cambridge: Harvard University Press, 1982.

Goodpasture, H. McKennie. *Cross and Sword*. Maryknoll, NY: Orbis Books, 1989.

Hanke, Lewis. *Aristotle and the American Indians: A Study in Race Prejudice*. Bloomington: Indiana University Press, 1959.

Hefner, Robert (ed.). *Conversion to Christianity*. Berkeley: University of California Press, 1993.

Held, Virginia (ed.). *Justice and Care: Essential Readings in Feminist Ethics*. Boulder: Westview Press, 1995.

Hu-Dehart, Evelyn. *Missionaries, Miners, and Indians*. Tucson: University of Arizona Press, 1981.

Jonas, Hans. *The Imperative of Responsibility*. Chicago: University of Chicago Press, 1984.

Kay, Michele. "Map Maker Folds." *Austin American-Statesman*, April 21, 1996, pp. B-1 & 6.

Kennedy, J.S. *The New Anthropomorphism*. Cambridge: Cambridge University Press, 1992.

Krutch, Joseph Wood. *The Voice of the Desert*. New York: Morow Quill Paperbacks, 1955.

Langer, E. & R. Jackson (eds.). *The New Latin American Mission History*. Lincoln: University of Nebraska Press, 1995.

Lasch, Christopher. *The True and Only Heaven: Progress and Its Critics*. New York: W.W. Norton & Co., 1991.

Lears, Jackson. *Fables of Abundance: A Cultural History of Advertising in America*. New York: Basic Books, 1994.

Leggett, Mike. "Spoilsports try to ruin a sick boy's dream wish." *Austin American-Statesman*, May 16, 1996.

Loftin, Robert W. "The Morality of Hunting." *Environmental Ethics*, Vol. 6, No. 3 (Fall 1984), pp. 241-250.

McCarthy, Cormac. *The Crossing*. New York: Vintage Books, 1994.

McRae, Roswell. *The Humane Movement.* New York: Columbia University Press, 1910.

Meilaender, Gilbert. *The Theory and Practice of Virtue.* Norte Dame: University of Notre Dame Press, 1984.

Mighetto, Lisa (ed.). *Muir Among the Animals.* San Francisco: Sierra Club Books, 1986.

Miller, Harlan & William Williams (eds.). *Ethics and Animals.* Clifton, NJ: Humana Press, 1983.

Miller, Richard. *Interpretations of Conflict.* Chicago: University of Chicago Press, 1991.

Muir, John. *My First Summer in the Sierra.* New York: Penguin Books, 1987.

———. *The Yosemite.* San Francisco: Sierra Club Books, 1914.

Nash, Roderick. *Wilderness and the American Mind.* New Haven: Yale University Press, 1982, Third Edition.

Nelson, Richard. *The Island Within.* San Francisco: North Point Press, 1989.

Newmhan, Blaine. "A Living Museum." *Pacific Magazine,* January 28, 1996, pp. 8-15.

Nielsen, Leon. "The Truth About 'No-Kill' Animal Shelters." *Animal Talk,* Vol. 1, #2 (Summer 1987).

Niven, Charles D. *History of the Humane Movement.* London: Johnson Publications, 1967.

Orion, Winter 1996:

Kerasote, Ted. "To Preserve the Hunt." pp. 13-19.

Romtvedt, David. "Strange Communion." pp. 20-24.

Causey, Ann S. "What's the Problem with Hunting?" pp. 25-28.

Legler, Gretchen. "Gooseberry Marsh." pp. 29-33.

Owens, C., R. Davis, & B. Smith. "The Psychology of Euthanizing Animals: The Emotional Components." *Int. J. Stud. Ani.,* 2(1) 1981, pp. 19-26.

Pieper, Joseph. *The Four Cardinal Virtues.* Notre Dame: University of Notre Dame Press, 1965.

Porter, Eliot. *The Place No One Knew: Glen Canyon on the Colorado River.* Salt Lake City: Peregrine Smith Books, 1988.

Regan, Tom. *The Case for Animal Rights.* Berkeley: University of California Press, 1983.

BIBLIOGRAPHY

Renicke, Jeff. *Bears of Alaska in Life and Legend.* Boulder: Roberts Rinehart, Inc., 1987.

Rivera, Luis. *A Violent Evangelism: The Political and Religious Conquest of the Americas.* Louisville: Westminister/ John Knox Press, 1992. Citation from: Beatriz Pastor. *Discurso Narrativo de la Conquista de America.* La Habana: Casa de las Americas, 1984.

Rodman, John. "The Liberation of Nature?" *Inquiry* 20 (Spring 1977), pp. 89-90.

Schor, Juliet, B. *The Overworked American.* New York: Basic Books, 1991.

Schultz, William. *The Humane Movement in the United States: 1910-1922.* New York: Columbia University dissertation, 1924.

Shannon, Thomas A. (ed.). *War or Peace.* Maryknoll, NY: Orbis Books, 1980.

Singer, Peter. *Animal Liberation.* New York: Avon Books, 1990, Revised Edition.

Smith Jane A. & Kenneth M. Boyd (eds.). *Lives in the Balance: The Ethics of Using Animals in Biomedical Research.* Oxford: Oxford University Press, 1991.

Spicer, Edward. *Cycles of Conquest.* Tucson: University of Arizona Press, 1962.

Stannard, David. *American Holocaust.* New York: Oxford University Press, 1992.

Taylor, Paul. *Respect for Nature: A Theory of Environmental Ethics.* Princeton: Princeton University Press, 1986.

Thomas, Keith. *Man and the Natural World: A History of the Modern Sensibility.* New York: Pantheon Books, 1983.

Thoreau, Henry David. *The Maine Woods.* New York: Harper & Row, 1987.

————. *Walden and Civil Disobedience.* New York: Airmont Publishing Co., 1965.

Tiscornia, Gary. "Letter From the Executve Director." Michigan Humane Society Newsletter (n.d.).

Traboulay, David M. *Columbus and Las Casas.* Lanham, MD: University Press of America, 1994.

Vitali, Theodore R. "Sport Hunting: Moral or Immoral?" *Environmental Ethics,* Vol. 12, No. 1 (Spring 1990), pp. 69-82.

Weber, Max. *The Protestant Ethic and the Spirit of Capitalism*. New York: Charles Scribner's Sons, 1958.

White, Kenneth. "Questioning the Question." *Shelter Sense*, Vol. 18, #1 (December 1994/January 1995), p. 2.

Wright, Phyllis. "Why We Must Euthanize." *Humane Society News*, Summer 1978.

INDEX

9 780965 728591

Printed in the United States
48019LVS00002B/277-300

9 780965 728591